Dr Mike Wilkinson is a barrister practising business and property law from 18 St John Street Chambers in Manchester. Whilst Mike's practice encompasses the traditional range of commercial chancery work, he has developed a particular interest in this field, establishing when those controlling a company will (or will not) be personally liable for harm caused to third parties for things they do (or intend to do) for the company.

to contract with[21]. Practitioners should check companies have complied with their trading disclosures not only for the commission of any criminal offences but if a company has not complied, they may well be at risk of being unable to enforce a contract by claim or counterclaim in accordance with s83 Companies Act 2006.

Chapter 4 – the relevant principles, rules and doctrines for upholding personal liability to third-party outsiders

It is a general principle of the law of tort that a person must be held responsible for his own acts and omissions which amount to a tort[22]. It is only in a contractual context that an agent can attribute his liability for breaching a contract to his principal in a way that exonerates such agent for liability for breach. The agent in such case has no liability because the contract is not theirs but that of their principal. But as a matter of agency law, personal liability is not extinguished merely because a person commits the tort whilst acting as an agent for their principal[23]. That agency relationship may give rise to the principal having vicarious liability for his or her agent, but vicarious liability is a form of secondary liability and not primary liability to be attributed to them.

The same principles apply also to directors acting for a company[24]. Separate legal personality does not exonerate a director from liability for the torts they commit even where they may be attributed to the Company. The attribution of an agent's acts to a company does not absolve the agent from his own liability[25]. It becomes a question of the extent of their involvement and participation in the tort.

---

[21] See Article 101 of Bowstead and Reynolds on Agency, Sweet & Maxwell, 22nd Ed citing *Holding v Elliott* (1860) 5 H. & N. 117.

[22] See for example the discussion on corrective justice in Honoré, Responsibility and Fault, Hart Publishing, 1999, p68.

[23] See Bowstead and Reynolds on Agency, Sweet & Maxwell, 22nd Ed, article 113.

[24] See the dictum of Cairns LJ in *Ferguson v Wilson* (1866) LR 2 Ch App 77, pp89-90. See also Chapter 9 of Bowstead and Reynolds on Agency, Sweet & Maxwell, 22nd Ed.

[25] See the observations of Dillon LJ in *Welsh Development Agency v Export Finance Co Ltd* [1992] B.C.C. 270 at p288, where the limits of the Said v Butt rule were discussed. See also *Standard Chartered Bank v Pakistan Shipping Corporation* [2003]

Personal liability can arise in one or more of two ways: where the controller commits all of the elements of the tort themselves; or where they commission it such as to become joint tortfeasor[26]. In either case, by committing a tort themselves or by actively participating in bringing it about the director will likely exceed their authority as mere agent[27]. Establishing liability is fact-sensitive and there is no simple formula for determining whether the requisite level of assistance and combination in some common design has taken place, but the assistance must be more than de minimis or trivial, and whilst a common design would normally be expressly communicated between the principal and the accessory, intention is something capable of being inferred[28].

---

1 A.C. 959 where the House of Lord clarified that a director's agency would not insulate a director from liability for deceit where they had backdated documents to obtain payment under a letter of credit.

[26] Liability as a joint tortfeasor can itself arise in two way: where two or more persons participate in some 'joint enterprise' or share some 'common design' to commit or commission a tort (see *Credit Lyonnais Bank Nederland NV v Export Credit Guarantee Department* [2000] 1 A.C. 486 HL); and/or where one instigates the commission of the tort by instructing, soliciting or inciting another or others to commit it (per Hobhouse LJ in the Court of Appeal in *Credit Lyonnais Bank Nederland NV v Export Credit Guarantee Department* [1998] 1 Lloyd's Rep.19 CA (Civ Div) which was affirmed on appeal by the House of Lords: [2000] 1 A.C. 486 HL). See also Clerk & Lindsell on Torts, Sweet & Maxwell, 32nd Ed, 4-04. In a company context, instigating the commission can be said to arise where a person 'intends and procures and shares a common design that the infringement takes place' they will be liable, per Lord Templemann, *CBS Songs v Amstrad* [1988] 2 All ER 484 at p496. Similar wording was adopted in *C Evans & Sons Ltd v Spritebrand ltd* [1985] 2 All ER 415 in which the court refused to strike out a claim against directors where there was evidence they might have procured or commissioned an infringement of copyright; and also *MCA Records Inc v Charly Records Ltd* [2001] EWCA Civ 1441 where it was held that a director would be jointly liable if he participated in the tort by directing infringement as that went beyond normal governance functions. For a case where a director was found not to have been sufficiently involved to procure a company's copyright infringement, see *Wirex Ltd v Cryptocarbon Global Ltd* [2021] EWHC 617 (IPEC).

[27] See *Chadwick LJ MCA Records Inc v Charly Records Ltd* [2001] EWCA Civ 1441 paras.49-50.

[28] See *Fish & Fish Ltd v Sea Shepherd UK, the Steve Irwin* [2015] UKSC 10, paras 20-24, 37-44, 55-61, 90-91.

Chapter 5 – types of torts giving rise to personal liability

Chapter 5 considers the types of torts and other causes of action where the courts have upheld personal liability including:

- *Procuring a breach of contract*: a director can be personally liable for procuring a breach of their company's contract where they exceed their authority by acting in bad faith towards their company. That can include exposing their company to potential liabilities, and even reputational harm. In *Antzuzis & Others v DJ Houghton Catching Services & Others* [2019] EWHC 843 (QB), for example, directors of a company that exploited their employees amongst other things by requiring the employees to work excessive hours, for less than the minimum wage were considered to act in bad faith towards their company by potentially exposing the company to claims and liabilities. They could thus be sued by their employees in tort for losses caused by procuring a breach of their employment contracts[29].

- *Negligence causing pure economic losses:* directors can be liable on an action for negligence causing pure economic losses where they have voluntarily assumed responsibility to protect the claimant from suffering such losses[30]. That commonly arises in a professional negligence context out of negligent mis-statements, but it is not limited to such contexts[31]. An assumption of responsibility, whilst difficult to prove[32], may arise where:

---

[29] See *Antzuzis & Others v DJ Houghton Catching Services & Others* [2019] EWHC 843 (QB).

[30] See *Williams v Natural Life Health Foods Ltd* [1998] 1W.L.R. 830 HL; *Hedley Byrne & Co Ltd v Heller & Partners Ltd* [1964] A.C. 465. But different principles apply if the negligence causes damage to property or to the person of if the alleged negligence really involves fraud or some economic tort including the tort of deceit: see for example *Noel v Poland* [2001] 2 B.C.L.C. 645 per Toulson J.

[31] Per Lord Sumption in *Playboy Club London Ltd v Banca Nazionale del Lavoro S.p.A.* [2018] UKSC 43 at [6]. And also *Henderson v Merrett Syndicates Ltd* [1995] 2 A.C. 145.

[32] See for example *Partco Group Ltd v Wragg* [2002] 2 B.C.L.C. 323 where making of statements relating to a takeover bid without any personal assurances was not enough to give rise to assumption of responsibility. But see *Fairline Shipping Corp v Adamson*

(1) the advice is required for a purpose, whether particularly specified or generally described, which is made known, either actually or inferentially, to the adviser at the time when the advice is given;

(2) the adviser knows, either actually or inferentially, that his advice will be communicated to the advisee, either specifically or as a member of an ascertainable class, in order that it should be used by the advisee for that purpose; (3) it is known either actually or inferentially, that the advice so communicated is likely to be acted upon by the advisee for that purpose without independent inquiry, and (4) it is so acted upon by the advisee to his detriment.[33]

- *Injury to property or person:* a person running a company may carry out activities that give rise to a personal duty of care to prevent injury or damage to third parties. Whilst the involvement of a company may negate a duty of care on the part of those running it, the ordinary principles for establishing a duty of care apply. Therefore situations involving a foreseeable risk of harm in circumstances of close proximity generally give rise to a duty of care being owed, and the fact such duty can be attributed also to a company does not necessarily negate the directors from also being liable[34]. Directors might thus be liable for causing personal injury whilst placing workers in a dangerous working environment[35], for damage to customer property whilst responsible for safekeeping their goods[36],

---

[1975] 1 Q.B. 180· where assumption of responsibility has been successfully argued in a case where director of a warehousing company was considered to have assumed personal responsibility to customers where he wrote a letter on his personal notepaper in the first person singular offering to store the Claimant's goods in his own premises in circumstances where the director wanted the storage to be his own venture and not that of the company; and see also *Morgan Crucible Co Plc v Hill Samuel Bank* ltd [1991] 1 All ER 148 where the Court of Appeal allowed an amended plea to be advanced against directors who allegedly made misrepresentations intended to be relied upon to a party making a takeover bid.

33 See *Caparo Industries Plc v Dickman* [1990] 2 A.C. 605 at 638C-E.

34 Per Viscount Haldane in *Lennard's Carrying Co Ltd v Asiatic Petroleum Co Ltd* [1915] A.C. 705.

35 See *Lewis v Boutilier* (1919) 52 D.L.R. 383; *Berger v Willowdale AMC* (1983) 145 D.L.R. (3d) 247.

36 See *Fairline Shipping Corp v Adamson* [1975] Q.B. 180 QBD.

for crashing a motor vehicle being driving for the company[37], and for running a ship aground when it was unseaworthy due to defective boilers[38]. In similar ways the law is also willing to impose a duty of care on a parent company to those dealing with its subsidiary[39].

- *Causing waste to property*: directors were held responsible for actions done on behalf of their company which led to third-party property being damaged. In *Mancetter Developments Ltd v Garmanson Ltd* [1986] Q.B. 1212 a director of a tenant company was liable in waste for causing his company to remove industrial machinery without making good holes made in the walls for the installation of fans and pipes.

- *Conversion:* where a controller themselves commit the act of conversion[40] or they procure others in their company to do it, they can be liable on an action for conversion[41], but they will typically have to have control of the goods and deny the true owner's claim to the goods upon notice of it[42].

- *Passing off and copyright infringement*: a director will be liable where he 'procured of or commissioned' copyright infringement by others in his or her company and he or she cannot escape liability by

---

[37] See *Microsoft v Auschina Polaris* (1996) 71 F.C.R. 231 at 242.

[38] See *Lennard's Carrying Co Ltd v Asiatic Petroleum Co Ltd* [1915] A.C. 705.

[39] See *Chandler v Cape Plc* [2012] EWCA Civ 525. Such duty can be imposed where there is a similarity of business, some actual or expected superiority of knowledge on the part of the parent company, actual or constructive foresight on the parent company's part of risk and harm and actual or constructive knowledge of reliance by the subsidiary on the intervention of the parent company. See also *Okpabi v Royal Dutch Shell* [2021] UKSC 3 and also *Vedanta Resources plc v Lungowe* [2019] UKSC 20 the Supreme Court was willing to uphold parent company liability or so-called 'value chain' liability and to impose duties of care on parent company controllers without involving any piercing of the corporate veil.

[40] See *Thunder Air Ltd v Hilmarsson* [2008] EWHC 355 (Ch).

[41] See for example *Caparo Industries Plc v Dickman* [1990] 2 A.C. 605 at 638C-E.

[42] See Article 114, Bowstead and Reynolds on Agency, Sweet & Maxwell, 22nd Ed.

arranging for the company he controls to commit the breach[43]. Liability commonly arises too in passing off cases[44].

- *Deceit:* a director that knowingly makes a false representation intending an outside third party to rely on it will be personally liable on an action for deceit where that outside third party acts in reliance on it and suffers losses[45]. In this context, a false representation can include a statement about a company's creditworthiness which induces a customer to enter into a transaction when the director knows the company cannot meet its obligations[46]. The mere signing of a contract can itself constitute the misrepresentation by impliedly representing that the company is able to meet its payment obligations when the person signing it knows for a fact it cannot[47]. A statement that money invested in a company will be used for a specific purpose can also give rise to a deceit when the misrepresenting director intends to use the money to repay existing debts[48]. Care must be taken in advancing any action in deceit to identify the correct directors that made the misrepresentations as in cases involving multiple directors, innocent co-directors who are not involved in making the representations will not be liable for the deceit of their co-directors[49].

- *Conspiracy:* a director can be liable for conspiring to cause losses to a third party, including planning to fold a company or strip it of

---

[43] See *C Evans & Sons Ltd v Spritebrand ltd* [1985] 2 All ER 415; also *MCA Records Inc v Charly Records Ltd* [2001] EWCA Civ 1441.

[44] See for example *Global Crossing Ltd v Global Crossing Ltd* [2006] EWHC 2043 (Ch).

[45] See *Standard Chartered Bank v Pakistan National Shipping Corp* [2003] 1 B.C.L.C. 244 where it was held that a director who acted on behalf of his company and made fraudulent misrepresentations to a bank to obtain payment would be liable along with his company for that misrepresentation.

[46] See *Lindsay v O'Loughlane* [2010] EWHC 529 (QB), but see also the formality requirements for representations relating to character as discussed in that case and arising under s6, the Statute of Frauds Amendment Act 1828.

[47] See *Context Drouzha Ltd Wiseman* [2007] EWCA Civ 1201.

[48] See *Edgington v Fitzmaurice* (1885) 29 ChD 459.

[49] See *Cargill v Bower* (1878) 10 ChD 502. But they may be liable if they participate as joint tortfeasors or as a part of a conspiracy.

assets[50], and such liability for conspiracy may be capable of being attributed to the company itself at least in civil law so that the corporate personality is a co-conspirator involved (at least notionally) in the collusion for the purposes of establishing conspiracy of the director[51]. A claimant can sue for losses caused by a conspiracy where it can be shown that two or more persons combined to perform acts which were unlawful or which although not unlawful were done with the predominant intent of causing injury[52].

- *Unlawful means tort:* a director can be personally liable to an outside third party for using unlawful means towards his or her own company to cause economic losses not to the company (or not just to the company) but to that outsider[53]. Primarily this claim is based on the principles upheld by the House of Lords in *OBG Ltd v Allan* [2007] UKHL 21; [2008] A.C. 1.

- *Dishonest assistance:* a director of a company that assists or procures his company to act deliberately in breach of trust, or a fiduciary

---

[50] See *Palmer Birch (A Partnership) v Lloyd* [2018] EWHC 2316 (TCC), where two individuals conspired to liquidate a company to avoid the company having to pay the claimants under a contract and were liable for unlawful means conspiracy (the unlawful means being inducing breach of contract by the company without justification).

[51] See *Belmont Finance Corp Ltd v Williams Furniture Ltd* [1979] Ch 250; *Yukong Line Ltd of Korea v Rendsburg Investments Corp of Liberia (No 2)* [1998] 1 W.L.R. 294. But see *R v McDonnell* [1966] 1 Q.B. 233 for the principles arising under the common law for the crime of conspiracy. But note the fact that liability is attributable to the company does not exonerate the director as co-conspirators, although an ignorant fellow director acting in good faith and not colluding will not be liable in conspiracy solely for doing something which might procure a breach of contract by his company (just as any agent would not be liable for procuring a breach by his principal: *Said v Butt* [1920] 3 K.B. 497) save perhaps with the exception that liability may potentially arise where equitable interests have already been acquired in property by third parties: see : *Telemetrix plc v Modern Engineers of Bristol (Holdings) plc* [1985] B.C.L.C. 213.

[52] See *Allen v Flood* [1898] A.C. 1 at 108.

[53] See Chapter 6 regarding asset-stripping and *Marex v Savilleja* [2020] UKSC 31 or for guidance on the tort: *OBG Ltd v Allan* [2007] UKHL 21; [2008] A.C. 1 and also Clerk & Lindsell on Torts, Sweet & Maxwell, 22nd Ed, 24-72.

duty[54], knowing of that breach[55], can be held liable for dishonestly assisting a breach of trust, or fiduciary duty, and they will be liable to pay equitable compensation, akin to damages, for all losses flowing from the breach of trust or fiduciary duty[56], including in cases where the company is insolvent[57].

- *Knowing receipt:* a director may be required to account as a constructive trustee if he or she lets their company be used for fraud that he or she has notice of by way of actual or constructive knowledge, including by turning a blind eye[58]. In any case, where a director takes receipt knowing it is trust property and/or converts trust property to their own use, they will be liable to account and there will be no time limit in limitation to recover such trust property[59].

---

[54] See *Fiona Trust & Holding Corporation v Privalov* [2010] EWHC 3199 (Comm).

[55] But nothing less than dishonesty will do: *Ivey v Genting Casinos UK Ltd (t/a Crockfords Club)* [2017] UKSC 67, [2018] A.C. 391, [2017] 10 WLUK 580 applied. But the dishonesty need not involve obvious, large transfers but might include a gradual erosion of trust assets by dissipation: *Trustor AB Ltd (Swedish Company) v Smallbone* [1968] 1 W.L.R. 1555.

[56] See *Royal Brunei Airlines Sdn Bhd v Tan* [1995] 2 A.C. 378.

[57] See *Royal Brunei Airlines Sdn Bhd v Tan* [1995] 2 A.C. 378, [1995] 5 WLUK 382.

[58] See *Shell International Trading Co Ltd v Tikhonov* [2010] EWHC 1770 (QB) in which Jack J held the corporate veil could not prevent a defendant, a senior employee of Shell, from being held liable to account in respect of bribes received directly by a company he controlled. See also *Agip (Africa) Ltd v Jackson* [1991] 3 W.L.R. 116 (CA). In any case, the controller of a one-man company that arranges for a transfer to that company of assets in breach of trust will be liable personally for his company's knowing receipt on an action in dishonest assistance: see also *Trustor AB v Smallbone* [2001] W.L.R. 1177.

[59] See s21 Limitation Act 1980 and *JJ Harrison (Properties) Ltd v Harrison* [2002] 1 B.C.L.C. 162 and *First Subsea Ltd v Balltec Ltd* [2017] Civ 187). The time period for fraudulent breach of trust in knowing receipt is different to that for dishonest assistance. Absent fraud or concealment being discovered or reasonably discoverable under s32, by analogy to s21, limitation on an action for dishonest assistance will be 6 years: see *Gwembe Valley Development Co Ltd v Kosby* [1998] 2 B.C.L.C. 613.

- *Bribery and secret commissions:* a director can be personally liable to account for a bribe he or she receives for a company[60].

Chapter 6 – Asset-stripping

In addition to any conspiracy to defraud[61], a director may also incur personal liability when stripping a company of its assets in three common scenarios.

The first is where an asset-stripper helps themselves to the assets of a company with the intention of prejudicing creditors. In such case, the asset-stripper may be personally liable for committing an unlawful means tort[62].

The second is where the company itself enters into an undervalue transaction purposefully to defraud its own creditors. Where an asset-stripper causes his company to enter into an arrangement for example to transfer assets to another party (or themselves) for an undervalue with the purpose of avoiding creditors, the court has powers to reverse the transaction or to order the recipient to pay compensation in relief[63].

---

[60] See *Shell International Trading Co Ltd v Tikhonov* [2010] EWHC 1770 (QB). Jack J also held the that corporate veil could not prevent a defendant, a senior employee of Shell, from being held liable to account in respect of bribes received directly by a company he controlled. Here an impeachable bribe has been paid, a claimant is entitled not only to that bribe but can also rescind any transaction arising out of it as of right, and an impeachable bribe may include a secret commission: see *Wood v Commercial First Business Ltd* [2021] EWCA Civ 471. The Court of Appeal provided clarity on secret commission cases by replacing the need for any agency arrangement with a test concerned only with some obligation or expectation that the intermediary would give disinterested and impartial advice, information or recommendations. The Court of Appeal cast some doubt on the distinction between fully secret and half secret commissions by finding there was an entitlement to rescission in a case where information had been provided to suggest a commission may be payable when one had in fact been paid.

[61] In *Palmer Birch (A Partnership) v Lloyd* [2018] EWHC 2316 (TCC), two individuals conspired to liquidate a company to avoid the company having to pay the claimants under a contract and were liable for unlawful means conspiracy (the unlawful means being inducing breach of contract by the company without justification).

[62] See *Marex v Sevilleja* [2020] UKSC 31.

[63] See s423 Insolvency Act 1986.

The third is the phoenix situation. It arises where the first company is liquidated but the asset-stripper starts up a new company carrying on using the name of the liquidated company without permission to do so. In such situations, those running the newco can be personally liable unless they comply with legislation permitting the newco to acquire the former company's trading name or they obtain permission[64].

Chapter 7 – Liability in proceedings

Those running a company can be personally liable in proceedings in three common situations.

First, the courts may require a party other than a claimant to pay security for the defendant's costs under r25.14CPR if satisfied it is just to make such order in all of the circumstances. That can arise where a director has contributed to paying the claimant's costs[65] and a failure to furnish documents relating to such funding can be treated as 'deliberate reticence' and lead to adverse inferences being drawn[66].

Second, those running a company may be ordered to pay the costs of proceedings that involve their company under s51 of the Senior Courts Act 1981. Whilst such non-party costs orders are exceptional, and they are only to be made where the court considers it just in all of the circumstances, they can be made, for example, where company controllers have: derived personal advantage from the litigation[67]; or pursued speculative litigation or incurred unreasonable costs by improperly arguing a case[68]. And it is not necessary to show that the director has acted in bad faith, or in abuse of the court's process or involved himself in some other impropriety[69]. The non-party will

---

[64] See s217, Insolvency Act 1986.

[65] See the judgment of Lord Brown in *Dymocks Franchise Systems (NSW) v Todd* [2004] 1 W.L.R. 2807 (PC) (costs) at paras. 24-25.

[66] See *SARPD Oil International Ltd v Addax Energy SA* [2016] EWCA Civ 120.

[67] See *Brampton Manor (Leisure) v McLean* [2007] EWHC 3340 (Ch). See also *Secretary of State for Trade and Industry v Aurum Marketing Ltd* [2002] B.C.C. 31.

[68] See *Goodwood Recoveries Ltd v Breen* [2006] 1 W.L.R. 2723.

[69] See *Secretary of State for Trade and Industry v Aurum Marketing Ltd* [2002] B.C.C. 31.

however need to be joined under r46.2 CPR and adequate notice given to ensure an opportunity to respond.

Third, those controlling a company may be committed for contempt of court and contempt may arise, for example, where: they have aided and abetted a company to commit a breach of court order; or they knowingly cause their company to avoid paying a judgment debt or to breach a court order; or they do not take reasonable steps to ensure compliance; or they are criminally responsible for interfering with the course of justice for example by deliberately frustrating the purpose of an order[70].

Chapter 8 – Liability imposed by statute

It is not surprising that the main statutes imposing liability upon directors are the Companies Act 2006, the Insolvency Act 1986, the Companies Directors Disqualification Act 1996 and various pieces of tax legislation. But there is also a wide range of other areas where statute imposes personal liability upon company controllers, including: employment law, housing law, and environmental law.

Chapter 8 considers some of the more common instances where statute imposes liability on company controllers for example: the Bribery Act 2010, the Data Protection Act 2018, the Environmental Protection Act 1990; the Equality Act 2010, the Financial Services and Markets Act 2000, the Health and Safety at Work Act 1974 and the Housing Act 2004.

It considers for example causes of action which might be brought against company controllers for misinformation in their Environmental Social Governance (ESG) reporting, or for breach of data protection obligations or breach of competition law.

It also considers not only statute imposing personal liability in civil law, but also some of the statutes that result in personal criminal liability, and when statutory duties can be enforceable by third parties.

---

[70] See *Attorney General v Punch Ltd* [2003] 1 A.C. 1046.

Chapter 9 – the conclusions and implications for practitioners

The concluding chapter summarises when third-party outsiders can hold those running a company personally liable for their involvement in wrongdoing causing them harm:

- Contract law will not give rise to liability for a corporate agent provided the company is the proper party.

- The agent will also not be liable in the tort of procuring a breach of contract unless they acted in bad faith to the company.

- Where the company is apparently the proper party to a contract or appears to own property in its right, veil-piercing or veil-lifting may be relevant, according to the tests of concealment or evasive interposition.

- Lifting the veil will be appropriate where upon scrutiny of the underlying facts the Court can be satisfied that the company is not the true actor and any transactions putatively in favour of the company are really shams or do not negate the reality that the company is the controller's agent or nominee holding on trust.

- Piercing the veil may be appropriate where there is an existing restriction or liability that is being evaded by the subsequent interposition of a company but it should only be resorted to where other relationships, principles or causes of action are unavailable.

- Outside of contract, it is a question of proving the controller's involvement in committing or commissioning the tort.

- It is not necessary to prove fraud upon an economic tort: directors can be personally liable on other causes of action too, including in negligence.

- In cases of negligence causing pure economic losses they are subject to the special assumption of responsibility test.

- Directors can be liable in negligence causing harm to property or person, for nuisance, for waste, and in equity for knowing receipt or dishonest assistance.

- In cases of conversion of property being dealt with by the company, there typically needs to be control of the goods and denial of the true owner's claim or the director will commission the conversion by being involved in bringing it about in bad faith[71].

- If all of the elements of the offence cannot be made out against a director, it may be possible to prove they commissioned the tort by being sufficiently involved in it to be joint tortfeasors.

- Joint tortfeasorship can arise in instances where one instigates another to commit a tort or where they both share a common design to bring it about.

- Stripping a company of assets to defraud a third party might give rise not only to claims in conspiracy, but on an action based on the unlawful means tort.

- The Insolvency Act 1986 also covers asset-stripping in phoenix situations where a liquidating company's name is re-used and also in cases where the company transfers assets to controllers at an undervalue to prejudice creditors.

- The fact directors may be personally liable, does not detract from the difficulties in establishing liability.

- Often decisions will be made in small companies without any formal minuting being produced recording decisions made at formally

---

[71] See Article 114, Bowstead and Reynolds on Agency, Sweet & Maxwell, 22nd Ed and *Thunder Air Ltd v Hilmarsson* [2008] EWHC 355 (Ch) and *Caparo Industries Plc v Dickman* [1990] 2 A.C. 605 at 638C-E.

convened meetings. Practitioners may thus find it hard formulating and advancing their cases with such informational asymmetry.

- Practitioners will thus want to consider the array of disclosure levers at their disposal including through resort to pre-action correspondence, pre-action disclosure applications or subject access data requests.

CHAPTER TWO

PIERCING AND LIFTING THE VEIL: INTERPOSING A COMPANY TO EVADE EXISTING RESTRICTIONS OR TO CONCEAL INVOLVEMENT

Introduction

Where a person incorporates a company with a view to shielding himself from liabilities incurred in running a business through the company, the company's separate legal personality should provide complete protection from personal liability, at least as far as the company's contractual liabilities are concerned. That is the principle of separate legal personality famously upheld in the case of *Salomon v Salomon* [1897] A.C. 22.

But it is now generally thought that the principle is subject to two exceptions in accordance with what Lord Sumption described as 'the concealment principle' and 'the evasion principle' in *Prest v Petrodel Resources Ltd* [2013] UKSC 34. On the one hand, the courts can 'lift' or 'look' behind a company's separate legal personality where it can be shown that a company is not the true actor, but has been interposed to conceal the involvement of its controller (the concealment principle).

On the other hand, if the company is the true actor, provided it can be shown that it was interposed by its controller to evade already existing obligations or legal restrictions the controller already fell under, then its separate legal personality may instead be 'pierced' (the evasion principle)[72].

It is important to clarify that piercing or lifting the veil involves disapplying a company's separate legal personality. It is very different to

---

[72] See *Prest v Petrodel Resources Ltd* [2013] UKSC 34.

holding controllers liable for some wrongdoing, whilst also recognising the existence of a company's separate legal personality. Lifting or piercing the veil is typically relevant in cases where a party needs to prove for example that property registered to a company or liabilities arising under a contract entered into by a company should be treated as belonging to the controller. Veil-piercing or lifting is not necessary however when an outsider has a cause of action to claim loss they have suffered by wrongdoing committed or commissioned by the controller.

It is also now tolerably clear that piercing the veil is different to lifting the veil, as veil-piercing involves the exercise of its own jurisdictional doctrine whereas lifting the veil involves merely finding the true actors involved and often concealed behind dealings. But despite plentiful cases raising veil-piercing, its jurisdictional basis remains controversial. Few authorities of the higher courts involve only an application of that piercing doctrine and Lord Sumption's narrow rationalisation of that doctrine in *Prest v Petrodel* was itself technically obiter. Amongst the authorities dealing with veil-piercing claims there is also a prevalence to resort instead to other causes of action and more clearly established legal doctrines which have clearer jurisdictional bases. *Prest v Petrodel* for example emphasised the exceptionality of the doctrine and Lord Neuberger and Lord Sumption have suggested it is a doctrine of last resort, available only where there are no other remedies[73]; or which can only come into play where other legal principles, relationships or causes of action cannot achieve the same result[74].

---

[73] In Prest, Lord Neuberger and Lord Clarke both suggested that the principle should only be applied where other principles are inapplicable. Whilst not expressly stating that the principle was of last resort, Lord Sumption suggested that Gilford Motor could have been decided on other grounds.

[74] Prest, para.35, per Lord Sumption: 'The principle is properly described as a limited one, because in almost every case where the test is satisfied, the facts will in practice disclose a legal relationship between the company and its controller which will make it unnecessary to pierce the corporate veil.' See also Lord Neuberger's suggestion at para.64 that the veil piercing cases could and should have been decided on other grounds.

Lord Neuberger even contemplated whether it was high time for the veil piercing doctrine to 'be given its quietus': para. 79.

Furthermore in the light of doubts expressed by the Supreme Court about the jurisdictional basis for piercing the corporate veil in *Hurstwood Properties Ltd v Rossendale Borough Council* [2021] UKSC 16[75], it remains to be seen how far lifting the veil and piercing the veil are limited to the concealment and evasion principles and how far they are discrete jurisdictional doctrines in their own right.

Typically, cases involving veil-lifting or veil-piercing will also involve allegations of fraud or trust or agency, and it may well be that the application of the doctrine is really just a misnomer and an incident of the courts granting relief where other causes of action and legal doctrines make way for the same relief.

This chapter considers veil piercing and lifting the veil by considering the main cases that have rationalised the jurisdictional doctrines and considering the implications for practitioners.

Salomon v Salomon [1897] A.C. 22 (HL)

Mr Salomon was a bootmaker who transferred his business into a small company which he ran and which he let members of his family take shares in. His company issued debentures to raise money, and subsequently defaulted on repayments. The liquidator sought to recover the balance form Mr Salomon arguing he should be responsible. Vaughan Williams J in the High Court considered the signatures of the family members subscribing to the company were mere 'dummies' and that the company was just Mr Salomon in another name or his alias or agent[76]. The Court of Appeal upheld that decision but on different rationale. Lindley LJ, expert on partnership law, considered that the company was really a

---

[75] See particularly paras.71-73. Lord Briggs and Lord Leggatt, with whom Lords Reed, Hodge and Kitchin all agreed, appears to question whether the courts even have a power to pierce the veil based on the evasion principle and they instead appear to query whether the evasion principle is not an incidence of piercing the veil but rather an application of agency law: see paras71 to 73.

[76] [1893] B 4793.

trustee for Mr Salomon 'improperly brought into existence by him to enable him to do what the statute prohibits'[77].

Lopes LJ and Kay LJ went even further and variously described the company as a 'myth' and a 'fiction' and said that the incorporation of the business by Mr Salomon had been a mere 'scheme' to enable him to carry on as before but with his personal liability for debt limited.

The House of Lords put paid to those agency and trust arguments unanimously overturning the decision. Lord Halsbury in particular considered there was no impropriety in incorporating a company to limit one's exposure to business liabilities and considered there was no trust, or agency or fraud made out on the facts. But at the same time as forcefully asserting that the veil of incorporation would protect those controlling a company from being liable for incorporating to limit their exposure, he also left the door open to veil-piercing arguments. He caveated that the status of a company's separate legal personality as distinct from that of its controlling applied in cases where there was 'no fraud and no agency and if the company is a real one and not a fiction or a myth'[78].

What is meant by 'no fraud', 'no agency' and the company being 'a real one and not a fiction or a myth' has since troubled lawyers and academics alike. Many a fine legal mind, and not only academics but also on the bench, have espoused justifications for piercing or lifting the veil wherever it was felt there was some form of abusive use of the company form, invoking its separate legal personality to masquerade some unconscionable or fraudulent behaviour. Lord Denning, for example, considered that courts had a discretion to lift the veil where the justice of the case required it[79], as did Robert Walker J[80] – comments which have since been roundly rebuked by the Supreme Court.

---

[77] [1895] 2 Ch. 323.
[78] [1897] A.C. 22 (HL), at p33.
[79] See *Littlewoods Mail Order Stores Ltd v IRC* [1969] 1 W.L.R. 1241, at p1254.
[80] See *Creasey v Beachwood Motors Ltd* (1992) B.C.C. 639.

Prest v Petrodel [2013] 2 A.C. 415

The long search for doctrinal clarity thankfully led to Lord Sumption's celebrated judgment in *Prest v Petrodel* [2013] 2 A.C. 415. In that case the Supreme Court opined, albeit obiter, that the courts cannot pierce the corporate veil unless the company is being used as a device to enable a controller to evade some existing legal obligation or restriction which they already fall under.

So, for example, where an outgoing employer is subject to his former employer's non-compete obligation, a company he interposes to compete with his employer can be restrained from competing by the courts[81]. Applying the evasion principle, the court can stop the controller of a company carrying on a business through the company he interposed to evade his existing obligation. Or where a landowner who has agreed to sell land to a party transfers it to his company, the company can be compelled to sell[82].

That rationalisation added much clarity to the law. No longer could litigants argue that a company's separate legal personality could be vitiated merely because it is just and equitable to do so.

Veil-piercing was not actually performed in Prest as it was instead found that the company held on trust for its controller. The justification for limiting the doctrine is technically obiter therefore and not all on the Supreme Court appeared to agree with it. Lady Hale in particular whilst concurring in the judgment gave a dissenting (also obiter) judgment doubting Lord Sumption's rationale:

92. I am not sure whether it is possible to classify all of the cases in which the courts have been or should be prepared to disregard the separate legal personality of a company neatly into cases of either concealment or evasion. They may simply be examples of the principle that the individuals who operate limited companies should not be allowed to take unconscionable advantage of the people with

---

[81] See *Gilford Motor Co Ltd v Horne* [1933] Ch.935, CA.

[82] See *Jones v Lipman* [1962] 1 W.L.R. 832 (Ch).

whom they do business. But what the cases do have in common is that the separate legal personality is being disregarded in order to obtain a remedy against someone other than the company in respect of a liability which would otherwise be that of the company alone (if it existed at all). In the converse case, where it is sought to convert the personal liability of the owner or controller into a liability of the company, it is usually more appropriate to rely upon the concepts of agency and of the "directing mind".

93. What we have in this case is a desire to disregard the separate legal personality of the companies in order to impose upon the companies a liability which can only be that of the husband personally. This is not a liability under the general law, for example for breach of contract. It is a very specific statutory power to order one spouse to transfer property to which he is legally entitled to the other spouse. The argument is that that is a power which can, because the husband owns and controls these companies, be exercised against the companies themselves. I find it difficult to understand how that can be done unless the company is a mere nominee holding the property on trust for the husband, as we have found to be the case with the properties in issue here. I would be surprised if that were not often the case.

It remains unclear after Prest whether veil-piercing is simply an exceptional doctrine that can be resorted to only in cases out of the ordinary or whether it is truly a doctrine of last resort[83]. Most cases involving the evasion principle also give rise to arguments about the

---

[83] In Prest, Lord Neuberger and Lord Clarke both suggested that the principle should only be applied where other principles are inapplicable. Whilst not expressly stating that the principle was of last resort, Lord Sumption suggested that Gilford Motor could have been decided on other ground. Also per Lord Sumption: 'The principle is properly described as a limited one, because in almost every case where the test is satisfied, the facts will in practice disclose a legal relationship between the company and its controller which will make it unnecessary to pierce the corporate veil.' para.35. See also Lord Neuberger's suggestion at para.64 that the veil piercing cases could and should have been decided on other grounds. And Lord Neuberger even contemplated whether it was high time for the veil piercing doctrine to 'be given its quietus' : see para.79.

concealment principle. The sense and purpose served by differentiating veil-piercing from lifting the veil has thus been doubted[84].

Whilst concealment cases were described by Lord Sumption as being 'legally banal'[85] no guidance was given around finding interposition to conceal the real actor. If that is meant to refer to cases where the company holds property on trust, it does not make the task of proving the trust any easier[86]. If it is a case that concealment might be found where a company is really the true agent of the controller, that does not lighten the burden of proving a company is the agent of its controller[87]. And if it is the case that concealment may arise because the company is a sham, it begs the question what the point of differentiating the different underling principles really is when they lead back to the same proposition, and makes it no easier to prove the sham[88].

---

[84] See *Hurstwood Properties Ltd v Rossendale Borough Council* [2021] UKSC 16 particularly para.73.

[85] See para.28.

[86] And whilst constructive and resulting trusts may survive the formality requirements of s2 <u>Law of Property Miscellaneous Provisions Act 1989</u>, if there is an express declaration of trust made upon a conveyance in favour of a company, a constructive trust or proprietary estoppel relying on a prior promise will be incapable of surviving the declaration of trust which would need to be set aside in its own right for fraud or mistake: see *Goodman v Gallant* [1986] Fam 106, CA and *Bahia v Sidhu* [2022] EWHC 875 (Ch). Similarly once a property is registered in a company's name, that will be conclusive unless the register is altered for mistake a fraud: s58 <u>Land Registration Act 2002</u>, schedule 4, paragraph 2.

[87] Lord Neuberger suggested the Gilford Motor case involved the company being the controller's agent see Prest, paras [60]–[74]. The task of proving agency is made especially difficult by the significance of the company's constitutional documents and the statutory effect of it having separate legal identity upon incorporation. No guidance is given for vitiating the constitutional documents which themselves set up the controller as the company's agent. Indeed, whilst Bowstead and Reynolds on Agency, Sweet & Maxwell, 22nd Ed suggest an agent will be liable to third parties where their principal is fictitious (see article 107) or the agent shown to be the real principal (article 108), there is scarce authority on what is involved in finding a company is the agent of its controllers.

[88] A sham transaction (which is perhaps not to be treated the same as a sham legal entity) was defined by Diplock LJ in *Snook v. London and West Riding Investments Ltd* [1967] 2 Q.B. 786, 802 as existing where parties execute documents or perform acts that are intended to give the appearance of legal rights and obligations being created that are different from what they intend. A company can be used to create

Hurstwood Properties Ltd v Rossendale Borough Council [2021] UKSC 16

Lord Sumption's narrow rationalisation has been given even further restrictive interpretation by the Supreme Court in the case of *Hurstwood Properties Ltd v Rossendale Borough Council* [2021] UKSC 16[89]. In that case, the Supreme Court considered that companies that had been incorporated to occupy property so as to assume liability for rates were not to be disregarded so as to allow the rates liability to fall on their controllers. Lord Briggs and Lord Leggatt, with whom Lords Reed, Hodge and Kitchin all agreed, questioned whether the courts even had a power to pierce the veil based on the evasion principle at all and they intimated that the evasion principle may not be an incidence of piercing the corporate veil but rather an application of agency law. They were also clear that they would not allow veil-piercing to impose a prospective liability instead of a retrospective liability:

71. Whether the evasion principle is needed or provides the best justification of cases such as Gilford Motor and Jones is itself open to debate. In his judgment in Prest Lord Neuberger of Abbotsbury said that the decision in the Gilford Motor case that an injunction should be granted against the company was "amply justified" on the basis that the company was Horne's agent for the purpose of carrying on the business (para 71); and that in Jones it was unnecessary to invoke the doctrine, as an order for specific performance against Lipman would have been sufficient by requiring him to procure that the company conveyed the property in question to the plaintiff (para 73). Baroness Hale expressed the view that in such cases it is usually more appropriate to rely on the concepts of agency and of the "directing mind". Lord Walker of Gestingthorpe questioned whether "piercing the corporate veil" is a coherent principle or rule of law at all, as opposed to simply a label used to describe the disparate occasions on which some rule of law produces apparent exceptions to the principle of the separate juristic

---

the appearance it is party to a transaction to mask who the real party is as in *Adams v. Cape Industries Plc* [1990] 2 W.L.R. 657 (HL).

[89] See paras.63 to 76.

personality of a corporate body (para 106). Although this is not the occasion for reaching any final view, we are inclined to share Lord Walker's doubts.

72. Even if there is an "evasion principle" which may in "a small residual category of cases" (per Lord Sumption) justify holding a company liable for breach of an obligation owed by its controlling shareholder, we are not ourselves convinced that there is any real scope for applying such a principle in the opposite direction so as hold a person who owns or controls a company liable for breach of an obligation which has only ever been undertaken by the company itself. At para 34 of his judgment in Prest, Lord Sumption said:

> It may be an abuse of the separate legal personality of a company to use it to evade the law or to frustrate its enforcement. It is not an abuse to cause a legal liability to be incurred by the company in the first place. It is not an abuse to rely on the fact (if it is a fact) that a liability is not the controller's because it is the company's. On the contrary, that is what incorporation is about.

He went on to refer to *VTB Capital plc v Nutritek International Corporation* [2013] UKSC 5; [2013] 2 A.C. 337, where it was argued that the corporate veil should be pierced so as to make the controllers of a company jointly and severally liable on the company's contract. Lord Sumption said that:

> the fundamental objection to the argument was that the principle was being invoked so as to create a new liability that would not otherwise exist. The objection to that argument is obvious in the case of a consensual liability under a contract, where the ostensible contracting parties never intended that any one else should be party to it. But the objection would have been just as strong if the liability in question had not been consensual.

73. That analysis, with which we respectfully agree, seems to us to leave very little room for reliance on the "evasion principle" to impose upon the controller of a company a fresh liability incurred by the company as distinct from its controller. But whether that is so or not, we think it clear that there is no scope for such a principle to operate in the present case. Liability for rates accrues from day to day. If the leases were effective to transfer the ownership of the demised properties for the purpose of the 1988 Act from the defendants to the SPVs (which is the premise on which the attempt to "pierce the corporate veil" becomes relevant), then in each case, from the date of the lease, the only person liable for business rates incurred thereafter was the SPV. Furthermore the interposition of the SPV had no effect at all on the liability of the landlord for rates up to the date of grant of the lease. Applying Lord Sumption's reasoning, it is not an abuse of the separate legal personality of the SPV to cause the liability for business rates to be incurred by the SPV by granting it a lease, nor to rely on the fact (if it is a fact) that the liability was not the defendant's because it was the company's. Nor can the evasion principle properly be invoked so as to create a liability on the part of the defendant that would not otherwise exist.

In the recent cases of *Okpabi v Royal Dutch Shell* [2021] UKSC 3, and *Vedanta Resources plc v Lungowe* [2019] UKSC 20 the Supreme Court's has also shown a willingness to engage in other ways of assessing liability of company controllers, rather than piercing the corporate veil, in particular by adopting a nuanced approach to assessing the parent company's liability for the acts or omissions of their subsidiary, according to the extent of their involvement in the de fact management of the activity in question.

Classic situations

What is clear from a look at the different authorities is that there are certain types of situations that commonly give rise to arguments about lifting or piercing the veil.

In criminal law, the concealment or evasion principles are regularly resorted to in cases concerning the proceeds of crime or confiscation proceedings. In *R v Sale* [2013] EWCA Crim 1306; [2014] 1 W.L.R. 663, a sole shareholder and director of a company that made a bribe to secure a valuable contract was made subject to a confiscation order in respect of the benefits of the bribe. His argument that the company was not a sham and he had not personally received a salary or dividends was rejected by Treacy LJ who considered the concealment principle to apply and him to be the true actor as the activities of the company were 'so interlinked as to be indivisible'[90] and the court was entitled to 'discover the facts which the existence of the corporate structure would otherwise conceal so as properly to identify the appellant's true benefit'[91].

In insolvency situations, office-holders will regularly find assets transferred to companies to evade detection or liabilities. In *Wood v Baker* [2015] EWHC 2536 (Ch), a trustee's application to freeze the assets held by various companies controlled by a bankrupt was granted by HHJ Hodge QC who accepted that the corporate veil could be pierced as the companies appeared not to be legitimate businesses but 'fronts' for the bankrupt, who had interposed them to evade his disclosure duties under s333 of the Insolvency Act 1986. He also suggested that they were arguably agents or nominees for the bankrupt.

In family law, piercing or lifting the veil is also regularly argued. In *Akhmedova v Akhmedov* [2018] EWFC 23, Haddon-Cave J was willing to pierce the veil to enforce an order for payment of £350,000 against a company owning a yacht which was controlled by the party subject to the order. Whether there was a need to pierce the veil is somewhat moot, given findings were made also that the assets were held on trust for the controller in that case[92]. Indeed, piercing the veil was considered unnecessary in *Prest v Petrodel* [2013] UKSC 34, where a divorcing husband who had acquired a property in the name of an interposed

---

[90] Para.40.
[91] Para.43.
[92] See paras.49 and 57.

company he controlled as he was treated as being the true owner of those assets anyway.

In an employment or contract context, outgoing employees or independent contractors are routinely subject to confidentiality obligations or to restraint of trade or non-compete obligations the company's separate personality can arguably be pierced[93].

In a property law context, a party that has contracted to sell land to another who transfers it to a company to evade being compelled to go through with the sale may be subject to injunction orders requiring payment on the footing the company is interposed to evade or frustrate his existing liabilities[94].

In a commercial context, the evasion of licensing restrictions also regularly crops up. Where a transport company would be unable to obtain a licence for its own vehicles if it made an application on its own behalf, the interposition of a subsidiary company that takes a transfer of the vehicles can also lead to the court refusing to treat parent and subsidiary as independent bodies, and considering them as one unit[95.]

Practical implications

It is moot whether the same outcomes would have been arrived at in each of the cases considered above had liability been analysed according to the principles of joint liability and causes of action against both company and controller in fraud.

---

[93] See *Gilford Motor Co Ltd v Horne* [1933] Ch.935, CA.

[94] See *Jones v Lipman* [1962] 1 W.L.R. 832 (Ch).

[95] See Palmer's company law, 2.1535, citing *Merchandise Transport Ltd v British Transport Commission (No. 1)* [1962] 2 Q.B. 173; [1961] 3 W.L.R. 1358; [1961] 3 All E.R. 495 CA; see also the observations of Lord Denning MR in *Littlewoods Mail Order Stores v Inland Revenue Commissioners* [1969] 1 W.L.R. 1241 CA (Civ Div) at 1254 and FG Films, Re [1953] 1 W.L.R. 483; [1953] 1 All E.R. 615 Ch D. See also *Linsen International Ltd v Humpuss Sea Transport Pte Ltd* [2011] EWHC 2339 (Comm); [2012] Bus. L.R. 1649; [2011] 2 Lloyd's Rep. 663).

It also remains to be seen whether the veil-piercing and lifting doctrines are doctrine of last resort which have their own jurisdictional bases or merely blunt instruments reached for when granting relief that would be justified under other causes of action. Instead of invoking veil-lifting or veil-piercing as their primary case, practitioners may wish to consider resorting to it as a fall-back argument.

Pleading out alternative cases in trust, agency or fraud requires considerable care. Chapter 5 considers what needs to be proved in fraud cases involving the various economic torts. As far as trust arguments are concerned, particular care should be taken not only to clarify how it is said the nominal relationship or resulting or constructive trust arises but also to deal with the consequences of any property disposition, registration or express declaration or deed of trust. Whilst constructive and resulting trusts may survive the formality requirements of s2 <u>Law of Property Miscellaneous Provisions Act 1989</u>, if there is an express declaration of trust made upon a conveyance in favour of a company, a constructive trust or proprietary estoppel relying on a prior promise will be incapable of surviving the declaration of trust which would need to be set aside in its own right for fraud or mistake: see *Goodman v Gallant* [1986] Fam 106, CA and Bahia v Sidhu [2022] EWHC 875 (Ch). Similarly once a property is registered in a company's name, that will be conclusive unless the register is altered for mistake a fraud: s58 Land Registration Act 2002, schedule 4, paragraph 2.

If it is to be argued that a company is an agent for the director, care should be taken to clarify how that relationship is said to have arisen and if by inference what facts lead to the same being drawn. Care will also be required to deal with and vitiate not merely any property or trust instruments, but also any company constitutional documents. In conjunction with such agency argument for example, it may be argued that the appointment of the controller as director is a mere sham[96] in the

---

[96] A sham transaction (which is perhaps not the same as a sham legal entity) was defined by Diplock LJ in *Snook v. London and West Riding Investments Ltd* [1967] 2 Q.B. 786, 802 (Eng. C.A.) to exist where parties execute documents or perform acts that are intended to give the appearance of legal rights and obligations being created that are different from what they intend.

context of the counter-agency, the company being used to create the appearance it is party to a transaction to mask who the real party is as in *Adams v. Cape Industries Plc* [1990] 2 W.L.R. 657 (HL).

Summary

- Veil-piercing or lifting is relevant for cases where a claimant needs to prove that property owned by a company or liabilities on a company contract ought instead to belong to the controller.

- Piercing or lifting the veil is not required to hold company controllers liable for harm they have caused outsiders where a cause of action other than a claim on the contract can be made out against them.

- Cases involving veil-piercing are likely to be rare and they should only arise where no sham, agency and trust is present.

- Veil-piercing may be limited to the evasion principle in which case it is hard to conceive of situations where other causes of action or relationships cannot also be made out.

- Where it can be said that the controller was interposing a company to evade his own obligations or restrictions, it is likely it can also be said that he has used his company as his own agent or he has used it to commit a fraud, for example, conspiring with his company to perform acts, which were either unlawful, or were done for the purpose of harming the claimant.

- Similarly, if concealment is present, it is hard to conceive of situations where trust or agency claims cannot also be advanced.

- Where it can be argued that the court should lift the veil and find that the controller was the true owner because he was hiding his assets in a company to avoid being identified as the true owner, it is likely it can also be said that the assets are really beneficially his and the company is holding as mere nominee on trust or that the transfer was made to defraud his creditors (as a part of a lawful means conspiracy or avoidance transaction subject to s423 of the <u>Insolvency Act 1986</u>).

- Practitioners will thus want to consider pleading out alternative causes of action and invoking other legal doctrines before resorting to readily to veil-piercing as a doctrine.

- And care should be taken where possible before adopting the terminology of 'veil-piercing' or 'lifting' when other relationships, principles and causes of action may be more fully articulated.

(b) a person dealing with a company—

(i) is not bound to enquire as to any limitation on the powers of the directors to bind the company or authorise others to do so,

(ii) is presumed to have acted in good faith unless the contrary is proved, and

(iii) is not to be regarded as acting in bad faith by reason only of his knowing that an act is beyond the powers of the directors under the company's constitution.

(3) The references above to limitations on the directors' powers under the company's constitution include limitations deriving—

(a) from a resolution of the company or of any class of shareholders, or

(b) from any agreement between the members of the company or of any class of shareholders.

(4) This section does not affect any right of a member of the company to bring proceedings to restrain the doing of an action that is beyond the powers of the directors.

But no such proceedings lie in respect of an act to be done in fulfilment of a legal obligation arising from a previous act of the company.

(5) This section does not affect any liability incurred by the directors, or any other person, by reason of the directors' exceeding their powers.

(6) This section has effect subject to—

- section 41 (transactions with directors or their associates), and

- section 42 (companies that are charities).

This important provision presumes authority on the part of directors and helps to engage the company in dealings with third parties. Where directors lack actual authority to contract on behalf of a company, this provision typically presume it exists. As such, directors are unlikely to be personally liable upon a common law action for breach of warrant of authority because whilst they might have wrongly warranted they had authority when that was not the case, s40 ordinarily remediates any absence of authority so as to bind and engage the company.

It may conceivably remain possible for situations to arise whereby the directors might still remain liable on an action for breach of warrant of authority for example where the company is able to set aside the contract[103], but s40 appears to have radically reduced the scope for any such action. Whilst a company might sue the director for exceeding his authority, usually the company will be engaged with a third party who will be unable to proceed against the directors personally.

The proper party principle

Just because a company is in existence when a contract is made however and the person purporting to run it happens to be a director and intends to contract for the company does not mean that the company will necessarily be the proper party to the contracts entered into with third parties.

To ensure that third parties dealing with an agent acting for a company, the law has long required a high level of disclosure about the company's existence and involvement.

Being a mere abstraction, a company can only deal with the world through its human agencies. It stands to reason therefore that unless those parties make it clear that they represent the company, third parties will not know they are dealing with a separate legal personality.

The law has thus imposed rather stringent obligations on directors to disclose the fact that they are dealing for the company. Until 2006, the

---

[103] See *West London Commercial Bank v Kitson* (1884) 13 Q.B.D. 360.

position used to be that unless a company's name was fully disclosed in contractual dealings, the parties contracting on its behalf would be personally liable. That position prevailed at least since the Companies Acts 1856 until the Companies Act 2006 which abrogated the old s349(4) of the Companies Act 1986.

The old s349(4) of the Companies Act 1986 was widely considered to be an arbitrary rule of law. It provided that directors would be personally liable upon any promissory note, endorsement, or order for money or goods in which the company's name was not fully disclosed. If in a contract or order a director thus referred to their company's trading name but not to its proper registered name or if the director even missed off the word 'limited' at the end of the company's registered name, the position under the old-s349 used to be that the director would be personally liable, and that was so even if the counter-party was not in any way mis-led be the omission or failure[104].

That inflexible rule provided by s349 of the Companies Act 1985 was jettisoned, by the Companies Act 2006 which introduced a new regime of trading disclosure requirements.

The Companies Act 2006 imposed criminal liability on directors for failing to disclose details of their company. Instead of providing for automatic personal liability like the old-s349, it allowed the courts to resort to property party principle to determine whether the company was sufficiently disclosed so as to be engaged, whilst also introducing limits on how far a company could enforce a contracts where the company's details had not been disclosed.

Under s1206 of the 2006 act it is an offence to fail to give trading disclosures of any requirements passed under s82, including the Company, Limited Liability Partnership and Business (Trading Disclosures) Regulations 2015 SI 2015/17 and the Companies (Trading Disclosures) Regulations 2008. These regulations are all too often honoured in the breach. And those advising companies, or third parties

---

[104] See *Scottish & Newcastle Breweries Ltd v Blair* (1967) SLT 72.

dealing with them, would do well to check for compliance with trading disclosures. It is a relatively straightforward exercise to check what details are provided about a company on its stationery, websites, email footers, pro-forma and contractual documents. It is surprising to see how little this criminal liability is discharged and how widely offences are being committed.

If a company does not comply with its trading disclosure obligation, there can be other repercussions. Proceedings to enforce a right arising out of a contract 'made in the course of a business in respect of which the company was, at the time the contract was made, in breach of its disclosure obligations' can be dismissed under s83 of the Companies Act 2006 which provides:

83 Civil consequences of failure to make required disclosure

(1) This section applies to any legal proceedings brought by a company to which section 82 applies (requirement to disclose company name etc) to enforce a right arising out of a contract made in the course of a business in respect of which the company was, at the time the contract was made, in breach of regulations under that section.

(2) The proceedings shall be dismissed if the defendant (in Scotland, the defender) to the proceedings shows—

(a) that he has a claim against the claimant (pursuer) arising out of the contract that he has been unable to pursue by reason of the latter's breach of the regulations, or

(b) that he has suffered some financial loss in connection with the contract by reason of the claimant's (pursuer's) breach of the regulations,

unless the court before which the proceedings are brought is satisfied that it is just and equitable to permit the proceedings to continue.

(3) This section does not affect the right of any person to enforce such rights as he may have against another person in any proceedings brought by that person.

That embargo falls short of imposing personal liability upon directors but it may provide a defence to a third party sued by a company in breach of its trading disclosure obligations where some inability to sue or loss results from the non-disclosure within the meaning of s82(2)(a) or (b). Further section 83 suggests that it is not merely the contract or relevant order which must comply with trading disclosures but any document in the course of relevant business. Practitioners would do well to check every missive, email, letter and piece of publicity, including websites, receipts, orders or invoices to see what trading disclosures are made. All too frequently directors fail to be circumspect and a failure to comply with their trading disclosure obligations, however apparently unimportant, may well prevent them from bringing a claim, or counterclaim unless the court considers it just and equitable to permit the proceedings, for example because it is satisfied that third parties have not been misled.

If a company's details are not sufficiently disclosed by a director, he runs the risk instead of becoming personally liable upon the contract, and that may be so even if he describes himself as a director[105]. Where the contract is in writing, and the company is named as a party and a director signs on its behalf, the company will be party to it. Where, however, the director signs in his own name failing to stipulate the company's name clearly or at all, unless it can be shown upon construction that the other contracting party should be taken to know he was dealing with a company the director could be personally liable on the contract. It will be a question of construction.

The parole evidence rule can operate in favour of finding directors personally liable. Where the terms merely refer to a director's name and not to his company, extrinsic evidence is typically inadmissible to prove that the parties discussed dealing with a company[106]. Provided that an

---

[105] See *McCollin v Gilpin* (1881) 6 Q.B.D. 516.
[106] See Article 100 of Bowstead and Reynolds on Agency, Sweet & Maxwell, 22nd Ed.

objective construction of the written contract does not show that the company was a party, extrinsic evidence to the contrary will be inadmissible.

Rules of construction often require the clearest of words to be used before implicating a company as a contracting party. Mere reference to the fact of a directorship or a passing reference to a company or a company's trading name in a contract may well be insufficient. For example, the words 'We, the undersigned, three of the directors, agree to repay £500 advanced by A to the company', were insufficient to implicate the company impliedly referred to by the 'three directors'[107].

Similarly, the clearest of words are often required before a director will be considered to have contracted in a dual capacity. In *Manches LLP v Freer* [2006] EWHC 991 (QB) for example a contract entered into with a company was found not to also have been entered into personally by the director despite providing for a personal guarantee because clear words were not used at the end of the contract to explain that the director was entering into the contract both in the capacity as director of the company and personally.

These principles of construction are even more stringent when construing deeds[108]. So a person who on a deed 'signed as agent for and on behalf of CIC' was still personally liable, notwithstanding that 'CIC' was the name of a French company, because its full corporate title was not provided[109].

Extrinsic evidence is admissible however to prove who the proper party to a contract was where there is ambiguity on the written contract as to who such party was. But self-serving evidence suggesting that a party was fully informed about the company's existence will likely be treated with suspicion where other written documents fail to clarify the company's

---

[107] See illustration (2) under Article 99 of Bowstead and Reynolds on Agency, Sweet & Maxwell, 22nd Ed, citing *McCollin v Gilpin* (1881) 6 Q.B.D. 516, and also *H.O. Brandt & Co v H.N. Morris & Co* [1917] 2 K.B. 784).

[108] See Article 102, Bowstead and Reynolds on Agency, Sweet & Maxwell, 22nd Ed.

[109] See illustration (2) for Article 102, Bowstead and Reynolds on Agency, Sweet & Maxwell, 22nd Ed, citing *Bailey v de Kerangat*, CA, December 7, 1993.

existence. So in *McKenzie O'Brien Butcher v Smith* [2009] EWHC 3925 (Ch) evidence of oral agreements about an intention to contract with the company was found to be improbable in the light of a supplier changing the customer's name on the invoice from the company to the director's name personally. The supplier's evidence was accepted that they had decided to contract personally with the director rather than the company having lost faith in the company's standing.

Similarly in the case of *Hamid v Francis Bacon Partnership* [2013] BLR 447 it was held that H's signature at the foot of a letter made him a contracting party, unless he qualified his signature or otherwise made it plain that the contract did not bind him personally, which he did not. The mere reference to a business name 'M', without any indication that this was the trading name of C or that C was a limited company, was not an effective qualification[110].

In *Tattersalls Ltd v McMahon* [2021] EWHC 1629 (QB) the High Court held that a director bidding at an auction was personally liable jointly and severally with his company. Even if the director had intended to contract only on the part of the company, without an agreement in place with the auction house by which they accepted the director was acting only as agent for a third party, their standard terms and conditions applied and the agent and any person they were acting for became jointly and severally liable and sections 40 (power to bind company) and 43 (company contracts) did not negate a director's liability as agent for the company.

When construing any written contract or admissible parole evidence, it is worth paying particular regard to whether there were any other breaches of trading disclosures and also what rules of attribution are provided for by the company's own constitution[111]. Articles of association commonly require board approval before a company enters into a contract[112].

---

[110] See paras 60-73 of *Hamid v Francis Bacon Partnership* [2013] BLR 447.

[111] See *Meridian Global Funds Management Ltd v Securities* [1995] A.C. 500 PC.

[112] See articles 7 to 16 of the model articles in schedule 1 to the Companies (Model Articles) Regulations 2008.

If, as is commonly the case, a director fails to disclose the fact they were acting as a company for example in various emails, or on their website, and fails to obtain board approval, the courts may have little sympathy with their bare assertion that the third party should have known they were acting as a company. After all directors not only have the power of disambiguation but will often have a positive obligation to clarify the company's involvement. When it comes to construing who objectively should be understood to have contracted, it can be difficult for directors to distance themselves from and disown the confusion they themselves have engendered by their own failures.

If a contract is oral and not written, or if it is part oral, part written, the question will not be one of objective construction as to what was reasonably understood by a person in the third party's positions, but rather a question of fact whether that party subjectively intended to contract with a company[113]. If your client does not know or intend to contract with a company at all, there will be no contract with the company, provided their evidence of subjective intent is accepted by a court.

Finally, it should be noted that s83 did not abrogate s26(2) of the <u>Bills of Exchange Act 1882</u> and so where a director signs a cheque or any negotiable instrument without stating the company's full name, he runs the risk of being personally liable on it, and such liability has arisen even where some attempt was made to refer to the company and the director's acting as agent, but where the company's name was not referred to in full[114].

Summary

- Pre-incorporation, where promoters enter into contracts for and on behalf of the company due to be incorporated, personal liability is likely to arise, but promoters can also sue upon those contracts.

---

[113] See Article 101 of Bowstead and Reynolds on Agency, Sweet & Maxwell, 22nd Ed citing *Holding v Elliott* (1860) 5 H. & N. 117.

[114] See *Rafanjan Pistachio Producers Co-operative v Reiss* [1990] B.C.L.C. 352.

- Contracts can be drafted to make provision for coming into existence of the company but there will need to be an actual novation agreement and express agreement, novation will not be readily inferred

- Directors can still incur personal liability on a contract according to the proper party principle where they fail to disclose the company's existence and involvement sufficiently to engage the company.

- In written contracts, the question of construing who the parties were will typically be straightforward: if the company is named as party and a director signs on its behalf there is unlikely to be any question; whereas if the company is not mentioned, the party signing on its behalf is likely to be bound, and they may have limited resort to extrinsic evidence.

- Only where it is ambiguous on the face of the contract whether or not the company was contracting will the courts allow resort to extrinsic evidence as to the proper party.

- Where the contract is oral or part-written and part-oral, subjective intent matters and it will be relevant who the third party understood themselves to be dealing with.

- Practitioners should check to see if companies have complied with their trading disclosures not only when construing who the proper party to the contract is, but to check whether a company is unable to enforce a contract under s83 and whether there are any criminal repercussions for trading disclosure failures.

CHAPTER FOUR

EXTRA-CONTRACTUAL LIABILITY: THE RELEVANT PRINCIPLES, RULES AND DOCTRINES FOR UPHOLDING PERSONAL LIABILITY

Introduction

A director of a company is not personally liable for torts committed whilst running their company merely because they happen to be a director at the time[115]. If they have acted within their constitutional role, transacting decisions for the company at board meetings, within their powers and duties as a director, it is unlikely that they will have personally participated in committing any tort and so the law will generally attribute responsibility for any acts they have done to the company in accordance with the rules of attribution[116]. If on the other hand a director actively participates in the tort by committing it themselves or by doing things in a way which show he or she 'intends and procures and shares a common design that the infringement takes place' they can be liable[117]. But before the law imposes personally liable, it must be shown that the director has

---

[115] See *Performing Right Society Ltd v Ciryl Theatrical Syndicate Ltd* [1924] 1 KB, CA. In that case, a play performed by a theatre group company in breach of copyright did not give rise to liability on the part of the directors who were not involved or cognisant.

[116] But see *T Oertli v EJ Bowman* [1956] R.P.C. 282 Ch D where Roxburgh J. held in effect that where the company was directed into a tortious policy, the directors who formulated the company's policy could be liable, suggesting that the mere approval of a particular tortious policy or decision entailing the commission of a tort at board level could be personally actionable on the basis of authorising, or directing or procuring the tortious conduct.

[117] Per Lord Templemann in *CBS Songs v Amstrad* [1988] 2 All ER 484 at 496.

been so involved and gone beyond acting within their authority as director[118].

This chapter explores what it means to exceed authority as a director and what participation in a tort is required for it to become actionable. It does so by exploring the principle of personal responsibility within an agency context, in other words situations when an agent will be liable even for acts they purport to commit for his or her principal, and the doctrines of joint tortfeasorship as well as the 'controlling mind' concept and the rules of attribution.

It identifies the three main situations in which the courts commonly uphold personal liability on the part of directors for extra-contractual wrongdoing preparing the ground for the discussion in the next chapter about what types of torts or other causes of action tend to result in personal liability being upheld.

The principle of personal responsibility

It is a general principle of the law of tort that a person will be held responsible for his own acts and omissions which amount to a tort[119]. As a matter of agency law, such personal liability is not extinguished merely because that person commits the tort whilst acting as an agent for another[120]. That agency relationship may give rise to the principal having vicarious liability for his or her agent, but vicarious liability is a form of secondary liability and not primary liability attributed to them. In other words, even if vicarious liability applies, the agent still remains primarily liable and personally responsible for any tort they have committed even if done whilst acting for their principal. This is the principle of personal responsibility.

---

[118] See *Chadwick LJ MCA Records Inc v Charly Records Ltd* [2001] EWCA Civ 1441 paras.49-50.

[119] See for example the discussion on corrective justice in Honoré, Responsibility and Fault, Hart Publishing, 1999, p68.

[120] See Bowstead and Reynolds on Agency, Sweet & Maxwell, 22nd Ed, article 113.

attribute to the company)[133]. The courts will not let a director benefit from blaming a company for his or her own wrongful acts.

In *Bilta (UK) Ltd v Nazir* (No 2) [2016] 1 A.C. 1 the Supreme Court clarified that different principles govern attribution as between a third party suing the company on the one hand and on the other between the director and the company:

(1) that in most circumstances the acts and state of mind of its directors and agents could be attributed to a company by applying the rules of the law of agency, but ultimately the key to any question of attribution was always to be found in considerations of context and the purpose for which the attribution was relevant; that where the purpose of the attribution was to apportion responsibility between a company and its agents so as to determine their rights and liabilities to each other, the result would not necessarily be the same as it would be in a case where the purpose was to apportion responsibility between the company and a third party; that where a company had been the victim of wrongdoing by its directors, or of which its directors had notice, that wrongdoing or knowledge of the directors could not be attributed to the company as a defence to a claim brought against the directors by the company's liquidators, in the name of the company and/ or on behalf of its creditors, for the loss suffered by the company as a result of the wrongdoing even where the directors were the only directors and shareholders of the company, and even though the wrongdoing or knowledge of the directors might be attributed to the company in other types of proceedings; and that, accordingly, the defence of ex turpi causa non oritur actio was not available to the defendant directors against the company's claim because the defendants' wrongful activities could not be attributed to the company in the proceedings brought by the liquidators (post, paras 7–9, 39–48, 84, 86–97, 181, 202, 208).

---

[133] See *Bilta (UK) Ltd v Nazir (No 2)* [2016] 1 A.C. 1 *per* Lord Neuberger at [7]; see also *Singularis Holdings Ltd v Daiwa Capital Markets Europe Ltd* [2020] 1 All ER 383).

Contributory negligence

For similar reasons, it is conceivable that a third party who is sued by a company for wrong they have done to the company might themselves sue the company's directors for contributing to those same losses in contribution proceedings. In Charter plc v Gawler [2008] Ch 313, a third party liable to a company for knowingly receiving company's money was able to argue that the directors should contribute towards repaying the company that money by failing to stop the transfers[134].

But a third party who is liable because of an agent's transgressions, cannot ordinarily reduce his liability by arguing that the principal was contributory negligent for such wrongdoing.

In *Corporacion Nacional del Cobre de Chile v Sogemin Metals Ltd* [1997] 1 W.L.R. 1396 it was held that contributory negligence was no defence to a claim for dishonest assistance. Where an action was founded on alleged bribery of the plaintiff's employee, the defendant could not, either in law or in equity, rely on the defence of contributory negligence to reduce his liability simply because the plaintiff could have intervened in the situation, but had not in fact done so.

Similarly, in *Goldtrail Travel Ltd v Aydin* [2014] EWHC 1587 (Ch) defendants that dishonestly assisted a company to breach a fiduciary duty could not claim a contribution from the company based upon the more culpable involvement of the controller being attributed to the company. Rose J held in that case that the director could not ratify his own dishonest assistance since : a) the Company was insolvent at the time the payments were made and the director therefore owed duties to the Company's creditors when making the payments (applying *Vivendi SA v Richards* [2013] EWHC 3006 (Ch), [2013] B.C.C. 771 applied, see bulletin 510); b) s239 Companies Act 2006 prohibited shareholders from ratifying breaches concerning themselves as director; c) s175(6) prohibited directors from authorising conflicts of interest involving themselves; and/or d) the inability of a sole director to ratify his own

---

[134] See para.74, per Arden LJ in particular.

wrongdoing in general meeting is not alleviated by the Duomatic principle (*Ultraframe (UK) Ltd v Fielding* [2004] RPC 479, at [40] applied).

Similarly, a third party that is sued by a company for breaching their duty to the company may be unable to argue that the company by reason of its own illegality cannot sue. In *Singularis Holdings Ltd (In Liquidation) v Daiwa Capital Markets Europe Ltd* [2019] UKSC 50 a bank had breached its *Barclays Bank Plc v Quincecare Ltd* [1992] 4 All E.R. 363, [1988] 2 WLUK 252 duty of care by transferring funds out of a company's account on the instructions of its sole shareholder and chairman. It was held that his fraudulent misappropriation could not be attributed to the company so as to preclude the company from suing the bank for breaching its duty:

> **Attribution** – The starting point was that a properly incorporated company had an identity and legal personality quite separate from that of its subscribers, shareholders and directors, *Salomon v Salomon & Co Ltd* [1897] A.C. 22, [1896] 11 WLUK 76 followed. Companies had to act through the medium of real human beings, so the issue was when the acts and intentions of real human beings were to be treated as the acts and intentions of the company, *Meridian Global Funds Management Asia Ltd v Securities Commission* [1995] 2 A.C. 500, [1995] 6 WLUK 307 and *Bilta (UK) Ltd (In Liquidation) v Nazir* [2015] UKSC 23, [2016] A.C. 1, [2015] 4 WLUK 410 followed, *Stone & Rolls Ltd (In Liquidation) v Moore Stephens (A Firm)* [2009] UKHL 39, [2009] 1 A.C. 1391, [2009] 7 WLUK 801 doubted.

The judge had found that the company was not a one-man company in the sense that the phrase was used in Stone & Rolls and Bilta. It had a board of reputable people and a substantial business. There was no evidence to show that the other directors were involved in or aware of S's actions; there was no reason why they should have been complicit in the misappropriation. The judge had made no error of law. She was also correct to say that there was no principle of law that where a company was suing a third party for breach of a duty owed to it by that third party, the fraudulent conduct of a director was to be attributed to the company if it was a one-man company. In her view, what emerged from Bilta was that the answer to any question whether to attribute the knowledge of the fraudulent director to the company was always to be found in consideration of the context and the purpose for which the attribution was relevant. That was correct, and if it was the guiding principle, then Stone & Rolls could finally be laid to rest, Bilta followed, Stone & Rolls doubted (paras 26-34). The instant context was the bank's breach of its Quincecare duty towards the company. The purpose of that duty was to protect the company against just the sort of misappropriation of its funds as had taken place. By definition, that was done by a trusted agent of the company who was authorised to withdraw its money from the account. To attribute the fraud of that person to the company would mean that really there would be no Quincecare duty or its breach would cease to have consequences. For the purpose of the Quincecare duty of care, S's fraud was not to be attributed to the company. However, even if it were, none of the bank's defences would succeed (paras 35, 38).

The rules of attribution

In *Meridian Global Funds Management Asia Ltd v Securities Commission* [1995] 2 A.C. 500 Lord Hoffmann considered the rules of attribution. He considered there to be primary and secondary rules of attribution. The primary rules determine who has the power to act on behalf of a company and bind it and are typically found in company law and the company's articles of association. So for example the unanimous consent or ratification of all shareholders in a decision will bind a company and will constitute a primary rule of attribution[135]. Ordinarily, a board of directors has authority to bind a company and if a company's business is conducted solely by the board by way of resolution at meetings, and provided the directors act within the scope of their authority according

---

[135] And such consent need not necessarily be expressed formally at a general meeting properly convened: see : re *Duomatic Ltd* [1969] 2 C 365; and also *Multinational Gas & Petrochemical Co v Multinational Gas & Petrochemical Services Ltd* [1983] Ch. 258.

to their articles and company law rules, their decision-making will generally be attributed to the company.

It is rare however for a company's articles to make provision for all of the decisions and actions taken by board room resolutions and so other rules of company law, and the law governing agency and authority also become relevant. Where decisions and responsibility for actions are delegated the rules of agency law and vicarious liability come into play and constitute what Lord Hobhouse described as secondary rules of attribution. Acts of persons who hold high office are generally attributed to the company such that their acts are considered to be those of the company (see *Lennard's Carrying Co Ltd v Asiatic Petroleum Co Ltd* [1915] A.C. 705 at 713-714 and also *Tesco Ltd v Nattrass* [1972] A.C. 153 at 170-171).

But where liability is attributed, whether through primary or secondary rules of attribution, it does not necessarily mean that the director will be exonerated from liability. The attribution of an agent's acts to a company does not have the effect of absolving the agent from his own liability. As was observed in *Standard Chartered Bank v Pakistan Shipping Corporation* [2003] 1 A.C. 959, a director's agency does not insulate them from liability for tort[136]. And as was alluded to by Dillon LJ in *Welsh Development Agency v Export Finance Co Ltd* [1992] B.C.C. 270 at p288 it is only in relation to the Said v Butt principle that an agent is shielded from liability where their acts can be attributed to their principal.

It is all too easy however to assume that an application of the identification doctrine will lead to the exclusion of an agent's personal liability. The fact that corporate agents can shield behind the corporate veil for their contractual dealings, makes it all too easy to believe they can be shielded from any liability. In their article 'Demystifying the Civil Liability of Corporate Agents' (2003) 62 CLJ 290 at 293, Neil Campbell

---

[136] In that case on an action in deceit for backdating documents to obtain payment under a letter of credit. The House of Lords corrected the Court of Appeal which had mistakenly applied the assumption of responsibility test to a case which did not involve a negligence claim to recover pure economic losses.

and John Armour rightly identify that as a thinking error, calling it the 'disattribution heresy'.

It remains to be seen how far the courts will exonerate or immunise directors in cases where their acts are attributed to or identified with the company. Doubtless there will be further cases considering how far the rules of attribution exclude a company controller from sharing liability. It may well be that in a company context, the test being developed and applied is not one according to the ordinary principles of joint tortfeasorship but according to some qualified version of that principle fashioned to account for the special phenomenon of the company's fictional personality. What is clear from a review of the authorities in which directors have been held liable and is that there are two ways in which directors are commonly found liable[137].

The two ways directors are personally liable

First, 'committing the tort': the courts have been willing to hold a director personally liable for his or her own tort where all of the elements of the tort can be said to have been committed by him or her personally. If they have committed the tort themselves it matters not whether they were acting in the course of business for the company at the time – although if they were so acting and within their authority, the company would also be vicariously liable for their torts[138]. In order to be liable for committing a tort, all of the elements of the tort must be shown to have been committed by the director personally and the rules of attribution for their acts or omission must fall short of exonerating them from taking responsibility for the same. How far acts can be attributed to a company such as to absolve an agent of liability is an area of law that remains to be developed and clarified. It may be as Dillon LJ suggested in *Welsh Development Agency v Export Finance Co Ltd* [1992] B.C.C. 270 at p288 that the attribution of an director's acts to a company will not dis-attribute so as to absolve the director from having liability themselves.

---

[137] See J.H. Farrar, "The Personal Liability of Directors for Corporate Torts" (1997) 9 Bond Law Review 102.

[138] See *Dubai Aluminium Co Ltd v Salaam* [2003] 2 A.C. 366, HL.

And second, 'commissioning the tort': where a person is 'bound up' in the commission of a tort[139], they will be a joint tortfeasors. In accordance with the principles of joint tortfeasorship, a director will be liable where he or she 'intends and procures and shares a common design that the infringement takes place'[140]. Or put differently, per Lord Buckmaster in *Rainham Chemical Works Ltd v Belvedere Fish Guano Co Ltd* [1921] 2 A.C. 465, at 467:

> If the company was really trading independently on its own account, the fact that it was directed by Messrs Feldman and Partridge would not render them responsible for its tortious acts unless, indeed, they were acts expressly directed by them. If ... those in control expressly directed that a wrongful thing can be done, the individuals as well as the company are responsible for the consequences.

There is no defined line and clear application of these two different tests. In finding liability on the part of directors sometimes judges allude to the general personal liability and in other cases they apply a direct and procure test.

What is clear is that there are a number of situations not only giving rise to frauds and economic torts where the courts have shown a willingness to uphold personal liability. Before exploring these different causes of action in Chapter 5, it is relevant to consider the significance of other common law rules.

The rule against recovery of pure economic losses

As with any claim for negligence, pure economic losses cannot be recovered unless there has been some voluntary assumption of responsibility on the part of the defendant to protect the claimant from

---

[139] See *Koninklijke Philips Electronics NV v Princo Digital Disc GmbH* [2003] EWHC 2589 (Ch). See also *Global Crossing Ltd v Global Crossing Ltd* [2006] EWHC 2043 (Ch) where it was held that even where a company was dormant when the action was later brought, a director and anyone else personally 'bound up' in the commission of a tort (such as a company secretary who helped to incorporate the defendant company to achieve the passing off in that case) will be joint tortfeasors.

[140] Per Lord Templemann *CBS Songs v Amstrad* [1988] 2 All ER 484, at p496.

suffering such losses[141]. That same principle applies in cases where directors of companies commit negligence [142] . Only where they voluntarily assume responsibility to a claimant may they be liable to them, unless they cause damage to property or injury to the person or commit some economic tort, including deceit[143]. That principle is all too easily misunderstood and should not be confused with any general proposition of law that directors cannot be liable for negligence. They can, but subject to assumption of responsibility test.

The rule against reflective losses

Another legal doctrine that has caused confusion until recently is the rule against reflective losses. Previously, where a creditor of a company had a cause of action against a director for losses they caused to the creditor which also reflected the losses that the company could also sue the director for, there used to be a rule of company law which prevented the creditor from pursuing a claim against the director for those losses as they were considered to be reflective losses or not losses separate and distinct to those that the company or any office-holder in an insolvency could recover for the company[144]. That rule has thankfully been overturned recently by the Supreme Court decision in *Marex v Sevilleja* [2020] UKSC 31 at least as far as non-shareholder creditors are concerned. It remains relevant for shareholder-creditors who are suing for damage to their shareholding, but not for the other creditors dealing with the company or strangers to the company who happen to encounter it who might bring the outsider actions considered by this book.

---

[141] See *Williams v Natural Life Health Foods Ltd* [1998] 1 W.L.R. 830 HL; *Hedley Byrne & Co Ltd v Heller & Partners Ltd* [1964] A.C. 465. But different principles apply if the negligence causes damage to property or to the person of if the alleged negligence really involves fraud or some economic tort including the tort of deceit: see for example *Noel v Poland* [2001] 2 B.C.L.C. 645 per Toulson J.

[142] See *Standard Chartered Bank v Pakistan International (No.2)* [2003] 1 A.C. 959 HL at [21], [41].

[143] See *Standard Chartered Bank v Pakistan Shipping Corporation* [2003] 1 A.C. 959.

[144] See the *Johnson v Gore Wood & Co* [2002] 2 A.C. 1.

Summary

- Whilst tortious acts or omissions of company controllers may sometimes be attributed to the company, such attribution of liability does not exempt the tortfeasor from taking responsibility themselves.

- The questions is one about proving the extent of their involvement and whether they have committed or commissioned a tort.

- They will have committed the tort if it can be shown that all of the elements of the cause of action are made out against them (whether or not they were acting for themselves or for their company).

- For negligence occasioning injury to person or property, there will need to be a duty of care owed by the director which typically arises where there is a foreseeable risk of harm in circumstances of close proximity, and the fact that such duty might also be attributed to a company does not necessarily negate the directors from also being liable[145].

- A controller will have commissioned a tort if it can be shown that they were joint tortfeasor.

- Joint tortfeasorship can arise where one incites another to commit a tort or where they share a common design[146].

- The rules of attributions place limits on the liability of an agent for breaching their company's contract: it is the principal and not the agent bound by the contract and liable to being sued on it.

- The law of agency also places limits on the tort of procuring a breach of contract by an agent, and also the tort of conversion, and in either

---

[145] Per Viscount Haldane in *Lennard's Carrying Co Ltd v Asiatic Petroleum Co Ltd* [1915] A.C. 705.

[146] See *Fish & Fish Ltd v Sea Shepherd UK, the Steve Irwin* [2015] UKSC 10.

case the agent must be exceeding their principal's authority acting in bad faith towards them before liability might arise.

- The rule against reflective losses no longer bars a third-party outsider from suing a director for harm they have caused where the company might also have a cause of action against the directors.

- The limitations on the recovery of pure economic losses in cases of negligence apply also to third-party outsider claims against directors.

CHAPTER FIVE

TYPES OF TORTS AND CAUSES OF ACTION GIVING RISE TO PERSONAL LIABILITY

Introduction

There are plenty cases in which the courts have held directors of a company to be personally liable to third parties outside of the company. This chapter looks at some of the main causes of action which have led to such liability being upheld. It is not intended to be exhaustive. Indeed, it will be immediately apparent that the types of torts leading to personal liability on outsider actions are not limited to fraud or more particularly the economic torts, but can cover other causes of action, such as personal injury, conversion, nuisance and breach of trust. The application of the principles, doctrines and rules discussed in the last chapter will undoubtedly lead to personal liability also being upheld on other causes of action not necessarily considered below. Those which are considered below however provide clear authority for finding personal liability on outsider actions.

Procuring a breach of contract

A director will not be personally liable for causing their company to breach its contracts, where he is acting bona fides towards his company within his authority as director[147]. But a director can be personally liable for procuring a breach where they exceed their authority by acting in bad faith to their company. Furthermore, directors that expose their company to liabilities including reputational harm may find it difficult to argue that they have acted in good faith within their authority.

---

[147] See *Said v Butt* [1920] 3 K.B. 497.

In *Antzuzis v DJ Houghton Catching Services* [2019] EWHC 843 (QB) directors of a company that exploited their employees in breach of the employee rights were liable personally for procuring a breach of contract. It was considered that requiring their company employees to work excessive hours, for less than the minimum wage, without holiday pay or bereavement leave and for amounts that were less than stated on their payslips, were not acts done in good faith towards their company but were liable to expose the company to claims and liabilities[148].

Negligence causing pure economic losses

Directors will not be liable for negligence causing pure economic losses unless there has been some voluntary assumption of responsibility on their part to protect the claimant from suffering such losses[149]. The same rule governing negligent claims for pure economic losses applies also in cases where directors of companies commit negligence[150]. Only where directors voluntarily assume responsibility to a party for their economic losses may they be liable – unless they cause damage to property or injury to the person or commit some other tort for which pure economic loss is recoverable, such as deceit[151] or any of the economic torts.

Assumption of responsibility cases commonly arise in connection with professional negligence claims[152] and typically they involve arguments about negligent advice or negligent mis-statements which have been relied upon by a claimant. The rule is not limited to those contexts

---

[148] See *Antzuzis & Others v DJ Houghton Catching Services & Others* [2019] EWHC 843 (QB).

[149] See *Williams v Natural Life Health Foods Ltd* [1998] 1 W.L.R. 830 HL; *Hedley Byrne & Co Ltd v Heller & Partners Ltd* [1964] A.C. 465. But different principles apply if the negligence causes damage to property or to the person of if the alleged negligence really involves fraud or some economic tort including the tort of deceit: see for example *Noel v Poland* [2001] 2 B.C.L.C. 645 per Toulson J.

[150] See *Standard Chartered Bank v Pakistan International (No.2)* [2003] 1 A.C. 959 HL at [21], [41]. See also *Williams v Natural Life Health Foods Ltd* [1998] 1 W.L.R. 830 HL, and for comparative law case: *Trevor Ivory Ltd v Anderson* [1992] 2 N.Z.L.R. 517 (New Zealand).

[151] See *Standard Chartered Bank v Pakistan Shipping Corporation* [2003] 1 A.C. 959.

[152] See for example *Caparo Industries Plc v Dickman* [1990] 2 A.C. 605 at 638C-E.

however but can cover all sorts of instances of alleged negligence causing economic losses[153].

Proving a voluntary assumption of responsible can be notoriously difficult[154]. Lord Oliver suggested in Caparo, that it may arise where:

> (1) the advice is required for a purpose, whether particularly specified or generally described, which is made known, either actually or inferentially, to the adviser at the time when the advice is given; (2) the adviser knows, either actually or inferentially, that his advice will be communicated to the advisee, either specifically or as a member of an ascertainable class, in order that it should be used by the advisee for that purpose; (3) it is known either actually or inferentially, that the advice so communicated is likely to be acted upon by the advisee for that purpose without independent inquiry, and (4) it is so acted upon by the advisee to his detriment.[155]

The inquiry into whether there is a voluntary assumption of responsibility is objective and looks to what is said or done by the director towards the tort victim[156]. A director of a warehousing company might also be considered to have assumed personal responsibility to customers where he wrote a letter on his personal notepaper in the first-person singular offering to store the Claimant's goods in his own premises in

---

[153] Per Lord Sumption in *Playboy Club London Ltd v Banca Nazionale del Lavoro S.p.A.* [2018] UKSC 43 at [6]. And also *Henderson v Merrett Syndicates Ltd* [1995] 2 A.C. 145.

[154] See for example *Partco Group Ltd v Wragg* [2002] 2 B.C.L.C. 323 where making of statements relating to a takeover bid without any personal assurances did not give rise to liability. But for cases where assumption of responsibility has been successfully argued see *Fairline Shipping Corp v Adamson* [1975] 1 Q.B. 180. Also see *Morgan Crucible Co Plc v Hill Samuel Bank ltd* [1991] 1 All ER 148 where the Court of Appeal allowed an amended plea to be advanced against directors who allegedly made misrepresentations intended to be relied upon to a party making a takeover bid.

[155] [1990] 2 A.C. 605 at 638C-E.

[156] See Lord Steyn, *Williams v Natural Life Health Foods Ltd* [1998] 1 W.L.R. 830 HL, 834-837.

circumstances where the director wanted the storage to be his own venture and not that of the company[157].

A director may become personally liable to a shareholder to give them impartial advice about rival bids the company has where he had agreed to act as their agent in negotiating a takeover bid[158].

Injury to property or person

A director's role may include being personally responsible for carrying out activities that give rise to a personal duty of care to prevent injury or damage to third parties, for example, piloting an aeroplane for a small private jet company or driving a coach for a small travel company. In such instances the director can be liable as a primary tortfeasor where it is shown he has been negligent. He cannot escape liability by saying it was not him but his company that crashed the plane or the coach.

A director may be personally liable therefore for causing personal injury whilst placing his workers in a dangerous working environment[159] or for damage to property where the director was responsible for safekeeping a customer's goods[160] or for crashing a motor vehicle he was driving for his company[161].

However, a director will not always be liable on such action where the involvement of the company negates a duty of care on his or her part. Situations involving a foreseeable risk of harm in circumstances of close proximity generally give rise to a duty of care being owed, pursuant to the ordinary principles of establishing a duty of care in negligence.

---

[157] See *Fairline Shipping Corporation v Adamson* [1975] Q.B. 180, per Kerr J at 186G-H.

[158] See *Paskin v Anderson* [2001] 1 B.C.L.C. 372 and *Re A Company 008699 of 1985* [1986] B.C.L.C. 382.

[159] See *Lewis v Boutilier* (1919) 52 D.L.R. 383; *Berger v Willowdale AMC* (1983) 145 D.L.R. (3d) 247.

[160] See *Fairline Shipping Corp v Adamson* [1975] Q.B. 180 QBD.

[161] See *Microsoft v Auschina Polaris* (1996) 71 F.C.R. 231 at 242.

In *Lennard's Carrying Co. Ltd v. Asiatic Petroleum Co. Ltd* 1915 A.C. 705, the House of Lords held that a director's liability for causing a loss of cargo because a ship ran aground when it was unseaworthy due to having defective boilers could be attributed to the company, when that director was its controlling mind such that both company <u>and</u> director could be primarily liable. As Viscount Haldane held:

> ...a corporation is an abstraction. It has no mind of its own any more than it has a body of its own; its active and directing will must consequently be sought in the person of somebody who for some purposes may be called an agent, but who is really the directing mind and will of the corporation, the very ego and centre of the personality of the corporation. .... It must be upon the true construction of that section in such a case as the present one that the fault or privity is the fault or privity of somebody who is not merely a servant or agent for whom the company is liable upon the footing respondeat superior, but somebody for whom the company is liable because his action is the very action of the company itself. It is not enough that the fault should be the fault of a servant in order to exonerate the owner, the fault must also be one which is not the fault of the owner, or a fault to which the owner is privy; and I take the view that when anybody sets up that section to excuse himself from the normal consequences of the maxim respondeat superior the burden lies upon him to do so.[162]

The courts have also held directors responsible for actions done on behalf of their company which have led to third-party property being damaged. In *Mancetter Developments Ltd v Garmanson Ltd* [1986] Q.B. 1212 a director of a tenant company was liable in waste for causing his company to remove industrial machinery without making good holes made in the walls for the installation of fans and pipes.

The law can impose a duty of care also on a parent company where there is similarity of business, some actual or expected superiority of knowledge on the part of the parent company, actual or constructive foresight on

---

[162] Per Viscount Haldane in *Lennard's Carrying Co Ltd v Asiatic Petroleum Co Ltd* [1915] A.C. 705.

the parent company's part of risk and harm and actual or constructive knowledge of reliance by the subsidiary on the intervention of the parent company[163].

It is possible that the courts may further develop the test of assumption of responsibility to negate liability for negligence in cases involving not only pure economic losses, but also where the negligence falls more properly within the company's sphere of activity. As things stand, however, the same test negating liability for pure economic losses appears to apply in the same way to company directors as any other instance where negligence causes pure economic losses, and it does not apply more generally to negate liability for other losses[164].

Conversion

An agent's control of goods will ordinarily be attributed to their principal and rarely gives rise to liability where they act in good faith on their behalf[165]. A director will also not ordinarily be liable for wrongful interference with goods or guilty of conversion on the basis that they are in control of the employees of the company that has custody and control of the goods[166]. If however the director has personal possession or control of the goods, even if they act in good faith, he or she can become liable for dealing with the goods without the true owner's authority if he or she is on notice of their claim to ownership[167]. He or she can also be liable

---

[163] See *Chandler v Cape Plc* [2012] EWCA Civ 525.

See also *Okpabi v Royal Dutch Shell* [2021] UKSC 3 and also *Vedanta Resources plc v Lungowe* [2019] UKSC 20 the Supreme Court was willing to uphold parent company liability or so-called 'value chain' liability and to impose duties of care on parent company controllers without involving any piercing of the corporate veil.

[164] Whilst Smith J considered arguments more generally about the proper allocation of risk between company and director in *Sainsbury's Supermarkets Ltd v Condek Holdings Ltd (formerly Condek Ltd)* [2014] EWHC 2016 (TCC) (see paragraph 33) the reason that claim against a director for negligence was dismissed in that case appears to have been the claim was for pure economic losses and there was found to be an absence of any voluntary assumption of responsibility for such losses.

[165] See Article 114 Bowstead and Reynolds on Agency, Sweet & Maxwell, 22nd Ed.

[166] See *Thunder Air Ltd v Hilmarsson* [2008] EWHC 355 (Ch).

[167] See *Powell v Hoyland* (1851) 6 Exch. 67; *Union Credit Bank v Mersey Docks & Harbour Board* [1899] 2 Q.B. 205.

for committing or commissioning the interference with the goods if they commit the conversion or incite others to do it. But liability will not ordinarily arise if he or she acts in good faith and does not deal with the goods[168] or their conduct falls short of repudiating the title of the true owner or he or she sells the goods which were not in his or her possession[169].

Where liability does arise there is no time limit to recover property in the director's possession or converted to their use[170] or where there was a fraudulent breach of trust and the director was privy to it[171].

Copyright infringement and passing off

A director cannot escape liability for infringing copyright or passing off by arranging for the company he controls to commit the breach. In *C Evans & Sons Ltd v Spritebrand ltd* [1985] 2 All ER 415 the court refused to strike out a claim against directors where there was evidence they might have 'procured or commissioned' the copyright infringement complained of. Similarly, in *MCA Records Inc v Charly Records Ltd* [2001] EWCA Civ 1441, it was held a director would be jointly liable if he participated in the infringement in a manner which went beyond his normal governance functions. Liability for passing off arose in *Global Crossing Ltd v Global Crossing Ltd* [2006] EWHC 2043 (Ch) not only for a director but any person 'bound up' in the commission of the tort such as the company secretary who helped to incorporate the company used for passing off[172].

---

[168] See *Caxton Publishing Co v Sutherland Publishing Co* [1939] A.C. 178 at 202.

[169] See Clerk and Lindsell on Torts (22nd ed), paras 17-17 and 17-73 onwards.

[170] See *JJ Harrison (Properties) Ltd v Harrison* [2002] 1 B.C.L.C. 162.

[171] See section 21 <u>Limitation Act 1980</u> and *First Subsea Ltd v Balltec Ltd* [2017] Civ 187.

[172] See for example *Global Crossing Ltd v Global Crossing Ltd* [2006] EWHC 2043 (Ch).

Deceit

A director can be personally liable where he or she fraudulently misrepresents matters which results in losses being caused to a third party who relies on the same as being truthful. Typically deceit cases involve statements of fact but they can include statements of opinion or intention if dishonestly held. A statement that a company is credit-worthy and able to honour its contractual commitments can even found an action in deceit: a director can be personally liable for the tort of deceit where he makes false representations about his company's creditworthiness to induce a customer to enter into transactions when he knows that the company cannot meet its payment obligations[173]. Indeed, the mere signing of a contract can itself constitute a misrepresentation where it impliedly represents that the company can meet its payment obligations when the person signing the contract knows for a fact that it cannot[174].

A statement that money invested in a company for example by purchasing bonds, would be used for a specific purpose can give rise to a deceit when the misrepresenting director dishonestly intends to use the money to repay existing debts[175]. A director who acted on behalf of his company and made fraudulent misrepresentations to a bank to obtain payment will be liable along with his company for that misrepresentation[176]. Falsifying documents required for a letter of credit to be issued can give rise to deceit[177].

Care must be taken around pleading actions in deceit and identifying which director committed a deceit in the case of potential involvement of multiple directors as directors will not be liable for the deceit of their co-directors[178] unless they are liable as accessory or co-conspirator.

---

[173] See *Lindsay v O'Loughlane* [2010] EWHC 529 (QB).

[174] See *Context Drouzha Ltd Wiseman* [2007] EWCA Civ 1201.

[175] See *Edgington v Fitzmaurice* (1885) 29 ChD 459.

[176] See *Standard Chartered Bank v Pakistan National Shipping Corp* [2003] 1 B.C.L.C. 244.

[177] See *Standard Chartered Bank v Pakistan Shipping Corpn* [2003] 1 A.C. 959.

[178] See *Cargill v Bower* (1878) 10 ChD 502.

Conspiracy

A claimant can sue for losses caused by a conspiracy where it can be shown that two or more persons combined to perform acts which were unlawful or which although not unlawful were done with the predominant intent of causing injury[179]. A director can be liable for conspiring with his company to cause losses to a third party and the liability for the conspiracy can be attributed to the company as well as to its human agencies[180]. The collusion can thus involve the company as a conspirator. Liability for conspiracy can even arise where directors plan to fold a company or strip it of assets. In *Palmer Birch (A Partnership) v Lloyd* [2018] EWHC 2316 (TCC), two individuals conspired to liquidate a company to avoid the company having to pay the claimants under a contract and were liable for unlawful means conspiracy (the unlawful means being inducing breach of contract by the company without justification).

The fact that liability is attributable also to the company does not exonerate the director as co-conspirator, although a director acting in good faith will not be liable in conspiracy solely for procuring a breach of contract by his company, just as any agent will not be liable for procuring a breach by his principal[181], perhaps with the exception that liability may arise where equitable interests have already been acquired in property by third parties[182].

Unlawful means tort

This action arises where one person uses unlawful means towards another with the object or effect of causing economic losses not to that person (or not just to that person) but to another person entirely[183]. This claim,

---

[179] See *Allen v Flood* [1898] A.C. 1 at 108.

[180] See *Belmont Finance Corp Ltd v Williams Furniture Ltd* [1979] Ch 250; *Yukong Line Ltd of Korea v Rendsburg Investments Corp of Liberia* (No 2) [1998] 1 W.L.R. 294. But see *R v McDonnell* [1966] 1 Q.B. 233 for the principles arising under the common law for the crime of conspiracy.

[181] See *Said v Butt* [1920] 3 K.B. 497.

[182] See *Telemetrix plc v Modern Engineers of Bristol (Holdings) plc* [1985] B.C.L.C. 213.

[183] See *OBG Ltd v Allan* [2007] UKHL 21; [2008] A.C. 1.

which was allowed in *Marex v Savilleja*, is considered in greater detail in the context of asset-stripping in the following chapter.

Breach of trust

Directors of companies that knowingly commit a breach of trust can be held liable for dishonestly assisting a breach of trust or fiduciary duty and liable upon an action for equitable compensation[184]. A director may be liable personally for dissipating money held by the company on trust[185].

It may also be possible for a director to be required to account as a constructive trustee[186] if he lets his company be used for fraud that he or she has notice of by way of actual or constructive knowledge including turning a blind eye[187]. So, the controller of a one-man company that arranges for a transfer to that company of assets in breach of trust can be liable personally for his company's knowing receipt on an action in dishonest assistance[188].

Equity imposes duties on a person not only who renders dishonest assistance in a breach of trust but also for dishonestly assisting any breach of fiduciary duty[189]. That can thus give rise to accessory liability on the part of a director who dishonestly assists a company to breach a fiduciary duty it owes to a third party, and it can also arise when the company is insolvent[190]. The requirements for liability are that there must have been a breach of trust or fiduciary duty and the defendant must have procured or assisted in that breach dishonestly[191]. The relief that can be claimed from the director rendering dishonest assistance is equitable

---

[184] See *Royal Brunei Airlines Sdn Bhd v Tan* [1995] 2 A.C. 378.

[185] See *Trustor AB Ltd (Swedish Company) v Smallbone* [1968] 1 W.L.R. 1555.

[186] See *Shell International Trading Co Ltd v Tikhonov* [2010] EWHC 1770 (QB) in which Jack J held the corporate veil could not prevent a defendant, a senior employee of Shell, from being held liable to account in respect of bribes received directly by a company he controlled.

[187] See *Agip (Africa) Ltd v Jackson* [1991] 3 W.L.R. 116 (CA).

[188] See *Trustor AB v Smallbone* [2001] W.L.R. 1177.

[189] See *Fiona Trust & Holding Corporation v Privalov* [2010] EWHC 3199 (Comm).

[190] See *Royal Brunei Airlines Sdn Bhd v Tan* [1995] 2 A.C. 378, [1995] 5 WLUK 382.

[191] Nothing less than dishonesty will do: *Ivey v Genting Casinos UK Ltd (t/a Crockfords Club)* [2017] UKSC 67, [2018] A.C. 391, [2017] 10 WLUK 580 applied.

compensation (akin to damages, save in all) for all losses flowing from the primary breach of duty by the fiduciary, and the same can be claimed notwithstanding that the company has been made insolvent[192].

Where a director is privy to a fraudulent breach of trust and converts the trust property to their use, there will be no time limit in limitation to recover trust property[193], but otherwise absent a situation where fraud or concealment was not discovered or reasonably discoverable under s32, by analogy to s21, limitation on an action for dishonest assistance will be 6 years[194].

In such cases, it will be no defence for the director to assert that their company was contributory negligent or mostly to blame[195] nor will they be able to rely on an illegality defence in an action brought by the company they control by saying that the company was involved in such illegality[196].

Even though a company will be dishonest vis-à-vis third parties when a director or a person who is the company's 'controlling mind or will' is dishonest, upon an action by the company against a director[197], illegality cannot be raised as a defence by a director on an action against him or her by the company, as their dishonest acts will not be attributed to the company when the company itself is the victim seeking compensation for harm done to it[198].

---

[192] See *Royal Brunei Airlines Sdn Bhd v Tan* [1995] 2 A.C. 378.

[193] See *JJ Harrison (Properties) Ltd v Harrison* [2002] 1 B.C.L.C. 162 and *First Subsea Ltd v Balltec Ltd* [2017] Civ 187).

[194] See *Gwembe Valley Development Co Ltd v Kosby* [1998] 2 B.C.L.C. 613.

[195] See *Corporacion Nacional del Cobre de Chile v Sogemin Metals Ltd* [1997] 1 W.L.R. 1396.

[196] See *Bilta (UK) Ltd (in liquidation) v Nazir* [2015] UKSC 23.

[197] See *Crown Dilmun v Sutton* [2004] EWHC 52 (Ch); [2004] 1 B.C.L.C. 468.

[198] The identification theory, which attributes the controlling mind and will of a director to a company, cannot be used against the company by such guilty director when acts are committed against the company itself: a director cannot negate liability for stealing money from a company by alleging that their dishonest intent becomes that of the company and/or that the company consents to the same: see *R. v McDonnell* [1966] 1 Q.B. 233; [1965] 3 W.L.R. 1138; [1966] 1 All E.R. 193 Assizes

Bribery and secret commissions

A director can be held personally liable to account for a bribe he or she receives for the company[199]. Where a secret commission or impeachable bribe arises, a claimant will be entitled not only to the payment of the bribe or commission but also to rescind any transaction as of right[200].

Summary

The courts have held those controlling companies personally liable to third-party outsiders upon the following causes of action:

- Procuring a breach of contract[201]

- Negligence causing pure economic losses, subject to a special assumption of responsibility[202]

(Bristol); *Attorney General's Reference (No.2 of 1982)* [1984] Q.B. 624 CA (Crim Div) at 640; *R. v Philippou (Christakis)* (1989) 5 B.C.C. 665; (1989) 89 Cr. App. R. 290; [1989] Crim. L.R. 585 CA (Crim Div); *DPP v Gomez (Edwin)* [1993] A.C. 442; [1992] 3 W.L.R. 1067; [1993] 1 All E.R. 1 HL.

[199] See *Shell International Trading Co Ltd v Tikhonov* [2010] EWHC 1770 (QB). Jack J held the corporate veil could not prevent a defendant, a senior employee of Shell, from being held liable to account in respect of bribes received directly by a company he controlled.

[200] See *Wood v Commercial First Business Ltd* [2021] EWCA Civ 471. The Court of Appeal provided clarity on secret commission cases by replacing the need for any agency arrangement with a test concerned only with some obligation or expectation that the intermediary would give disinterested and impartial advice, information or recommendations. The Court of Appeal cast some doubt on the distinction between fully secret and half secret commissions by finding there was an entitlement to rescission in a case where information had been provided to suggest a commission may be payable when one was in fact paid.

[201] See *Antzuzis & Others v DJ Houghton Catching Services & Others* [2019] EWHC 843 (QB).

[202] See *Williams v Natural Life Health Foods Ltd* [1998] 1 W.L.R. 830 HL; *Hedley Byrne & Co Ltd v Heller & Partners Ltd* [1964] A.C. 465. But different principles apply if the negligence causes damage to property or to the person of if the alleged negligence really involves fraud or some economic tort including the tort of deceit: see for example *Noel v Poland* [2001] 2 B.C.L.C. 645 per Toulson J. See also *Fairline Shipping Corp v Adamson* [1975] 1 Q.B. 180.

- Negligence causing injury to property or to the person[203]

- The tort of causing waste[204]

- The tort of conversion in cases of control and denial of title or bad faith[205] or commissioning the conversion[206]

- Copyright infringement[207] and passing off[208]

- Deceit[209]

- Conspiracy[210]

- Unlawful means tort[211]

- Dishonest assistance in a breach of trust or a fiduciary duty[212]

---

[203] See the judgment of Viscount Haldane in *Lennard's Carrying Co Ltd v Asiatic Petroleum Co Ltd* [1915] A.C. 705. See also *Lewis v Boutilier* (1919) 52 D.L.R. 383; *Berger v Willowdale AMC* (1983) 145 D.L.R. (3d) 247; *Chandler v Cape Plc* [2012] EWCA Civ 525.

[204] See *Mancetter Developments Ltd v Garmanson Ltd* [1986] Q.B. 1212.

[205] See Article 114, Bowstead and Reynolds on Agency, Sweet & Maxwell, 22nd Ed.

[206] See *Thunder Air Ltd v Hilmarsson* [2008] EWHC 355 (Ch). See also *Caparo Industries Plc v Dickman* [1990] 2 A.C. 605 at 638C-E.

[207] See *C Evans & sons Ltd v Spritebrand ltd* [1985] 2 All ER 415 ; also *MCA Records Inc v Charly Records Ltd* [2001] EWCA Civ 1441.

[208] See for example *Global Crossing Ltd v Global Crossing Ltd* [2006] EWHC 2043 (Ch).

[209] See *Standard Chartered Bank v Pakistan National Shipping Corp* [2003] 1 B.C.L.C. 244; *Lindsay v O'Loughlane* [2010] EWHC 529 (QB); Context *Drouzha Ltd Wiseman* [2007] EWCA Civ 1201; *Edgington v Fitzmaurice* (1885) 29 ChD 459; and *Cargill v Bower* (1878) 10 ChD 502.

[210] See *Palmer Birch (A Partnership) v Lloyd* [2018] EWHC 2316 (TCC) and *Belmont Finance Corp Ltd v Williams Furniture Ltd* [1979] Ch 250; *Yukong Line Ltd of Korea v Rendsburg Investments Corp of Liberia (No 2)* [1998] 1 W.L.R. 294.

[211] See Chapter 6 regarding asset-stripping and *Marex v Savilleja* [2020] UKSC 31 or for guidance on the tort: *OBG Ltd v Allan* [2007] UKHL 21; [2008] A.C. 1 and also Clerk & Lindsell on Torts, Sweet & Maxwell, 22nd Ed, 24-72.

[212] See *Fiona Trust & Holding Corporation v Privalov* [2010] EWHC 3199 (Comm).

- Knowing receipt[213]

- Bribery and secret commissions[214].

---

[213] See *Shell International Trading Co Ltd v Tikhonov* [2010] EWHC 1770 (QB) ; *Agip (Africa) Ltd v Jackson* [1991] 3 W.L.R. 116 (CA); *Trustor AB v Smallbone* [2001] W.L.R. 1177.

[214] See *Shell International Trading Co Ltd v Tikhonov* [2010] EWHC 1770 (QB).

later been interpreted) had gone too far and it unanimously ruled that a creditor of an asset-stripped company was not barred from suing the directors personally (unless they were also a shareholder as well, or would otherwise benefit from double recovery). Lord Sales (with whom Lady Hale agreed) gave a minority dissenting judgment, commenting obiter that the rule against reflective losses itself is not necessary at all and should be done away with altogether whether or not shareholders were concerned. The decision is thus important for removing what would otherwise be an impediment to creditors suing an asset-stripper personally.

(1) the first asset-stripping situation: an unlawful means tort

Marex v Savilleja was concerned with a cause of action based upon the tort of unlawful means. Marex alleged that Mr Savilleja intentionally caused loss to Marex by unlawful means namely by depleting his companies of the assets required to pay the judgment debts. It was argued that misappropriating the company money of sums needed for the company to comply with court orders was a tort or maliciously procuring violation of Marex's rights under the judgment of 25 July 2013 was a tort along the same nature said to be recognized in *Lumley v Gye* (1853) 2 E & B 216.

Primarily the claim was based on the principle recognised in *OBG Ltd v Allan* [2007] UKHL 21; [2008] A.C. 1. *In OBG Ltd v Allan* [2007] UKHL 21; [2008] A.C. 1 guidance was given around the tort which used to be referred to as 'unlawfully interfering with another's business' but which has more recently been redefined more generally as an 'unlawful means tort' [221]. The tort arises where one person uses unlawful means towards another with the object or effect of causing economic losses not to that person (or not just to that person) but to another person entirely[222].

Unlawful means tort is a rather undeveloped tort, or rather a tort whose boundaries are hard to define. The essence of the tort is said to be

---

[221] See *OBG Limited v Allan* [2008] A.C. 1, at 62.
[222] See Clerk & Lindsell on Torts, Sweet & Maxwell, 22nd Ed, 24-72.

deliberate interference with the claimant's interests in a party by using unlawful means to that party. It arises where a claimant has suffered damage in their relationship with a party which has been brought about intentionally or foreseeably by a defendant using unlawful means towards that party, and not the claimant themselves.

'Unlawful means' are typically acts against a third party which are themselves actionable by that third party[223]. Any breach of contract, tort, breach of statutory duty or equitable duty owed to that third party might thus qualify as unlawful means and the thing done to the third party by the defendant can be unlawful under the civil law or criminal law[224]. Not every unlawful thing will be actionable however even if the same causes losses which are intended to be caused[225]. Lord Brown and Lady Hale endorsed the following ratio of Lord Hoffman in OBG:

> [It] consists of acts intended to cause loss to the claimant by interfering with the freedom of a third party in a way which is unlawful against the third party and is intended to cause loss to the claimant; but it excluded acts which did not affect the third party's freedom to deal with the claimant

In order to be entitled to bring a claim for an unlawful means tort, the claimant must have an 'economic or financial interest' in the third party, and the unlawful means must cause a loss to their economic interests in that third party or harm their economic expectations. The defendant need not have a preponderant intention that such loss results: it will suffice if such loss is the inevitable effect of causing harm. So, even if unlawful means are employed for some ulterior motive, such as self-enrichment, it is likely to be caught by the tort, provided that the loss was an inevitable and foreseeable consequence[226].

Certain unlawful means, such as breach of some equitable duties, or breach of contract, appear to be more peripheral to the action than

---

[223] See *OBG Limited v Allan* [2008] A.C. 1, at 49.

[224] See *OBG Limited v Allan* [2008] A.C. 1, 162.

[225] See Clerk & Lindsell on Torts, Sweet & Maxwell, 32nd Ed, 24-74.

[226] See Street on Torts, Blackwell, 15th Ed, p371.

others[227]. Since procuring a breach of contract is its own tort, it is questionable whether the courts will expand the unlawful means tort to include directing a company to default on a contract, but if they do the status of *Said v Butt* [1920] 3 K.B. 497 will have to be dealt with.

In that case, Mr Butt was the director of the Palace Theatre. Mr Said, a wealthy Russian gentleman who had been critical of the theatre, had been banned from attending the theatre by Mr Butt. A friend of Mr Said's purchased a ticket on his behalf, and when Mr Said tried to attend he was refused entry. Mr Said sought to enforce the contract but he was not entitled to do so because at the time formation the intention of Mr Butt was not to contract with Mr Said and so no contract was found to have arisen. Additionally, the Court considered that a claim against Mr Said's agent for procuring a breach of contract could not be sustained. It held that a servant acting bona fides within the scope of his authority should not be liable in tort for procuring a breach of contract between his employer and a third person. The Said v Butt rule is not without controversy and criticism and it remains to be seen how the courts will qualify or shape this tort in the future.

Said v Butt did not involve asset-stripping however. Where the unlawful means is not simply procuring the company to default on a contract but misappropriating company property to render the company incapable of honouring its commitments, the elements of the tort may well be made out. That was indeed the position advanced in Marex v Sevilleja.

Unfortunately, the unlawful means tort remains controversial and of indeterminate ambit, as might well be expected from a tort which extends the right to sue from the immediate victim of a tort to a secondary party who was intentionally or inevitably also targeted. It remains to be seen how far the courts will permit this tort to be developed in connection with company controllers. Asset-stripping is an obvious area where this tort may arise.

(2) the second asset-stripping situation: transactions defrauding creditors

---

[227] See Clerk & Lindsell on Torts, Sweet & Maxwell, 32nd Ed, 24-79.

Where the company's assets are not taken but the company voluntarily transacts to deprive itself of its own assets, the court's powers to set aside or reverse the transaction under s425 of the <u>Insolvency Act 1986</u> can be engaged. They provide:

423. Transactions defrauding creditors.

(1) This section relates to transactions entered into at an undervalue; and a person enters into such a transaction with another person if—

(a) he makes a gift to the other person or he otherwise enters into a transaction with the other on terms that provide for him to receive no consideration;

(b) he enters into a transaction with the other in consideration of marriage or the formation of a civil partnership; or

(c) he enters into a transaction with the other for a consideration the value of which, in money or money's worth, is significantly less than the value, in money or money's worth, of the consideration provided by himself.

(2) Where a person has entered into such a transaction, the court may, if satisfied under the next subsection, make such order as it thinks fit for—

(a) restoring the position to what it would have been if the transaction had not been entered into, and

(b) protecting the interests of persons who are victims of the transaction.

(3) In the case of a person entering into such a transaction, an order shall only be made if the court is satisfied that it was entered into by him for the purpose—

(a) of putting assets beyond the reach of a person who is making, or may at some time make, a claim against him, or

(b) of otherwise prejudicing the interests of such a person in relation to the claim which he is making or may make.

(4) In this section "the court" means the High Court or—

(a) if the person entering into the transaction is an individual, any other court which would have jurisdiction in relation to a bankruptcy petition relating to him;

(b) if that person is a body capable of being wound up under Part IV or V of this Act, any other court having jurisdiction to wind it up.

(5) In relation to a transaction at an undervalue, references here and below to a victim of the transaction are to a person who is, or is capable of being, prejudiced by it; and in the following two sections the person entering into the transaction is referred to as "the debtor".

424 Those who may apply for an order under s. 423.

(1) An application for an order under section 423 shall not be made in relation to a transaction except—

(a) in a case where the debtor has been [F1made] bankrupt or is a body corporate which is being wound up or [F2is in administration], by the official receiver, by the trustee of the bankrupt's estate or the liquidator or administrator of the body corporate or (with the leave of the court) by a victim of the transaction;

(b) in a case where a victim of the transaction is bound by a voluntary arrangement approved under Part I or Part VIII of this Act, by the supervisor of the voluntary arrangement or by any person who (whether or not so bound) is such a victim; or

(c) in any other case, by a victim of the transaction.

(2) An application made under any of the paragraphs of subsection (1) is to be treated as made on behalf of every victim of the transaction.

425 Provision which may be made by order under s. 423.

(1) Without prejudice to the generality of section 423, an order made under that section with respect to a transaction may (subject as follows)—

(a) require any property transferred as part of the transaction to be vested in any person, either absolutely or for the benefit of all the persons on whose behalf the application for the order is treated as made;

(b) require any property to be so vested if it represents, in any person's hands, the application either of the proceeds of sale of property so transferred or of the money so transferred;

(c) release or discharge (in whole or in part) any security given by the debtor;

(d) require any person to pay to any other person in respect of benefits received from the debtor such sums as the court may direct;

(e) provide for any surety or guarantor whose obligations to any person were released or discharged (in whole or in part) under the transaction to be under such new or revived obligations as the court thinks appropriate;

(f) provide for security to be provided for the discharge of any obligation imposed by or arising under the order, for such an obligation to be charged on any property and for such security or charge to have the same priority as a security or charge released or discharged (in whole or in part) under the transaction.

(2) An order under section 423 may affect the property of, or impose any obligation on, any person whether or not he is the person with whom the debtor entered into the transaction; but such an order—

(a) shall not prejudice any interest in property which was acquired from a person other than the debtor and was acquired in good faith, for value and without notice of the relevant circumstances, or prejudice any interest deriving from such an interest, and

(b) shall not require a person who received a benefit from the transaction in good faith, for value and without notice of the relevant circumstances to pay any sum unless he was a party to the transaction.

(3) For the purposes of this section the relevant circumstances in relation to a transaction are the circumstances by virtue of which an order under section 423 may be made in respect of the transaction.

(4) In this section "security" means any mortgage, charge, lien or other security

This type of claim may be more appropriate where those controlling a company merely take its property, without engaging the company to formally agree to such transactions, as happened in Marex. In other words, it may be more apt for cases where the company formally approves transactions in favour of directors, shareholders or related parties for example where the asset-stripping is of a sophisticated nature perhaps buried under multiple formal agreements which have the verisimilitude of legitimacy, but which when unpicked are demonstrably determinantal to creditors and involve significant undervalue transfers in favour of company controllers or related parties.

The claim is not subject to insolvency proceedings[228]. And the cause of action does not create a statutory tort[229] although for the purposes of limitation it may be that it is treated as involving a breach of statutory duty for s32(2) of the Limitation Act 1980. The cause of action can have extra territorial scope[230].

---

[228] See *Re Baillies Ltd* [2012] EWHC 285 (Ch): The curative provision in r10.64 of the Insolvency Rules 2016 thus does not apply.

[229] See *Erste Group Bank AG v JSC* [2013] EWHC 2926 (Comm) per Flaux J.

[230] See *Orexim Trading Ltd v Mahavir Port and Terminal Private Ltd* [2018] EWCA Civ 1660.

The cause of action is useful because it can cover a wide range of transactions [231] and even dividends to shareholders which might otherwise have been lawful might be caught[232]. The elements of the claim are generally easier to prove than a conspiracy which requires injurious intent or unlawful actions. The requisite intention to make out a s423 claim is not fraudulent intent but merely that a motivating purpose that is prejudicial to creditors[233].

The transferor does not have to intend to prejudice the claimant individually and they may not even have had the claimant in particular in mind when entering into a transaction liable to prejudice creditors more generally[234]. The fact that a transferor enters into a transaction upon legal advice does not necessarily negate their prejudicial intent[235] and the courts can also waive privilege to ascertain motives[236].

However, the courts will generally require cogent proof of the significant undervalue, but the intention to defraud is often gathered and inferred from the lack of any good explanation for entering into such disadvantageous transaction.

The relief to be granted by the Courts is restitutionary in nature [237], and it is not intended to be punitive[238]. The Court enjoys a wide discretion to exercise the powers in s425 which themselves are extensive[239].

(3) the third asset-stripping situation: use of the phoenix

---

[231] See *Ailyan v Smith* [2010] BPIR 289.

[232] See *BTI 2014 LLC v Sequana SA* [2019] EWCA Civ 112.

[233] For a discussion on whether the purpose needs to be dominant or substantial and a consideration of the conflicting authorities see Sealy & Milman: Annotated Guide to the Insolvency Legislation 24th Ed, commentary on s423.

[234] See *Fortress Value Recovery Fund v Blue Skye Specialial Opportunities Fund* [2013] EWHC 14 (Comm) per Flaux J.

[235] See *Arbuthnot Leasing International Ltd v Havelet Leasing Ltd (No2)* [1990] B.C.C. 978.

[236] See *Barclays Bank v Eustice* [1995] 1 W.L.R. 1238.

[237] See *Johnson (Liquidator of Strobe 2 Ltd) v Arden* [2018] EWHC 1624 (Ch).

[238] See *Deansgate 123 LLP v Workman* [2019] EWHC 2 (Ch) per HHJ Eyre QC.

[239] See *Bataillon v Shone* [2016] EWHC 1174 (QB).

The final scenario clients may be faced with involve asset-strippers setting up a new company and continuing to trade. This is often referred to as the phoenix, the mythological bird that would burn itself on a pyre only to rise anew, reborn out of the ashes of its destruction.

The situation is governed by statute. The <u>Insolvency Act 1986</u> provides:

216 Restriction on re-use of company names.

(1) This section applies to a person where a company ("the liquidating company") has gone into insolvent liquidation on or after the appointed day and he was a director or shadow director of the company at any time in the period of 12 months ending with the day before it went into liquidation.

(2) For the purposes of this section, a name is a prohibited name in relation to such a person if—

(a) it is a name by which the liquidating company was known at any time in that period of 12 months, or

(b) it is a name which is so similar to a name falling within paragraph (a) as to suggest an association with that company.

(3) Except with leave of the court or in such circumstances as may be prescribed, a person to whom this section applies shall not at any time in the period of 5 years beginning with the day on which the liquidating company went into liquidation—

(a) be a director of any other company that is known by a prohibited name, or

(b) in any way, whether directly or indirectly, be concerned or take part in the promotion, formation or management of any such company, or

(c) in any way, whether directly or indirectly, be concerned or take part in the carrying on of a business carried on (otherwise than by a company) under a prohibited name.

(4) If a person acts in contravention of this section, he is liable to imprisonment or a fine, or both.

(5) In subsection (3) "the court" means any court having jurisdiction to wind up companies; and on an application for leave under that subsection, the Secretary of State or the official receiver may appear and call the attention of the court to any matters which seem to him to be relevant.

(6) References in this section, in relation to any time, to a name by which a company is known are to the name of the company at that time or to any name under which the company carries on business at that time.

(7) For the purposes of this section a company goes into insolvent liquidation if it goes into liquidation at a time when its assets are insufficient for the payment of its debts and other liabilities and the expenses of the winding up.

(8) In this section "company" includes a company which may be wound up under Part V of this Act.

217 Personal liability for debts, following contravention of s. 216.

(1) A person is personally responsible for all the relevant debts of a company if at any time—

(a) in contravention of section 216, he is involved in the management of the company, or

(b) as a person who is involved in the management of the company, he acts or is willing to act on instructions given (without the leave of the court) by a person whom he knows at that time to be in contravention in relation to the company of section 216.

(2) Where a person is personally responsible under this section for the relevant debts of a company, he is jointly and severally liable in respect

of those debts with the company and any other person who, whether under this section or otherwise, is so liable.

(3) For the purposes of this section the relevant debts of a company are—

(a) in relation to a person who is personally responsible under paragraph (a) of subsection (1), such debts and other liabilities of the company as are incurred at a time when that person was involved in the management of the company, and

(b) in relation to a person who is personally responsible under paragraph (b) of that subsection, such debts and other liabilities of the company as are incurred at a time when that person was acting or was willing to act on instructions given as mentioned in that paragraph.

(4) For the purposes of this section, a person is involved in the management of a company if he is a director of the company or if he is concerned, whether directly or indirectly, or takes part, in the management of the company.

(5) For the purposes of this section a person who, as a person involved in the management of a company, has at any time acted on instructions given (without the leave of the court) by a person whom he knew at that time to be in contravention in relation to the company of section 216 is presumed, unless the contrary is shown, to have been willing at any time thereafter to act on any instructions given by that person.

(6) In this section "company" includes a company which may be wound up under Part V.

Liability under s216 arises not only where the exact same name is re-used but where a similar name is used and it is not limited to the registered name but also covers trading names[240].

It is also not limited to situations involving the incorporation of a new company but can include existing companies for example in group company situations. For example, an existing company may use a name which becomes prohibited upon the liquidation of a related company or alternatively a company may later change its name or trading name to one which is or becomes prohibited[241].

Liability is limited to situations where the first company goes into insolvent liquidation. The personal liability is also limited to debts arising during the period when a director is involved in running a company reusing the prohibited name. But where personal liability arises, it extends not only to debts but to any other company obligations such as a liability on a claim for damages. It also applies not only to liabilities incurred by the person involved for their own personal acts but to any liabilities arising during the period of their involvement[242]. There is a presumption operating against a person who follows the instructions of another known to be contravening the restrictions on re-using prohibited names under s217(5).

The Courts have proven to be unsympathetic in allowing persons liable under s217 to seek contribution or indemnity. In *Revenue and Customs v Yousef* [2008] EWHC 423 (Ch) the Court refused to allow a right of indemnity between persons liable under s217 or between them and the company under the Civil Liability (Contributions) Act 1978. In *Thorne v Silverleaf* [1994] B.C.C. 109 the Court of Appeal considered it irrelevant to a defendant's liability under s217 that the claimant had aided. and abetted the defendant.

---

[240] See s216(2) and (6).
[241] See *Ricketts v Ad Valorem Factors Ltd* [2003] EWCA Civ 1706.
[242] See 217(1) and (3).

The courts do have a power to dispense with liability under s216)3) upon application but not retrospectively [243]. Any person found to have breached s216 cannot have their liability relieved under s1157 of the Companies Act 2006 [244]. Lack of managerial skills, commercial experience and/or funds have been held not to be relevant considerations for granting dispensation[245]. The Insolvency Rules 2016 also provide three categories where liability will not arise: including where a successor company buys the liquidating company and notice is given to creditors of the intended re-use of the name; where an application is made to the court within 7 days of the liquidation and the court grants leave within 6 weeks thereof; and where the second company has already been using the prohibited name for more than 12 months prior to liquidation whilst trading.

In particular the Insolvency Rules 2016 provide:

First excepted case

22.4.—(1) This rule applies where—

(a) a person ("the person") was within the period mentioned in section 216(1) a director, or shadow director, of an insolvent company that has gone into insolvent liquidation; and

(b) the person acts in all or any of the ways specified in section 216(3) in connection with, or for the purposes of, the carrying on (or proposed carrying on) of the whole or substantially the whole of the business of the insolvent company where that business (or substantially the whole of it) is (or is to be) acquired from the insolvent company under arrangements—

(i) made by its liquidator, or

---

[243] See *Re Neath Rugby Club Ltd v Cuddy* [2007] EWHC 1789 (Ch); *Re Bonus Breaks Ltd* [1991] B.C.C. 546.

[244] See *First Independent Factors & Finance Ltd v Mountford* [2008] EWHC 835 (Ch).

[245] See *Penrose v Official Receiver* [1996] 1 W.L.R. 482.

(ii) made before the insolvent company entered into insolvent liquidation by an office-holder acting in relation to it as administrator, administrative receiver or supervisor of a CVA.

(2) The person will not be taken to have contravened section 216 if prior to that person acting in the circumstances set out in paragraph (1) a notice is, in accordance with the requirements of paragraph (3),—

(a) given by the person, to every creditor of the insolvent company whose name and address—

(i) is known by that person, or

(ii) is ascertainable by that person on the making of such enquiries as are reasonable in the circumstances; and

(b) published in the Gazette.

(3) The notice referred to in paragraph (2)—

(a) may be given and published before the completion of the arrangements referred to in paragraph (1)(b) but must be given and published no later than 28 days after their completion;

(b) must contain—

(i) identification details for the company,

(ii) the name and address of the person,

(iii) a statement that it is the person's intention to act (or, where the insolvent company has not entered insolvent liquidation, to act or continue to act) in all or any of the ways specified in section 216(3) in connection with, or for the purposes of, the carrying on of the whole or substantially the whole of the business of the insolvent company,

(iv) the prohibited name or, where the company has not entered into insolvent liquidation, the name under which the business is being, or is to be, carried on which would be a prohibited name in respect of the person in the event of the insolvent company entering insolvent liquidation,

(v) a statement that the person would not otherwise be permitted to undertake those activities without the leave of the court or the application of an exception created by Rules made under the Insolvency Act 1986,

(vi) a statement that breach of the prohibition created by section 216 is a criminal offence, and

(vii) a statement as set out in rule 22.5 of the effect of issuing the notice under rule 22.4(2);

(c) where the company is in administration, has an administrative receiver appointed or is subject to a CVA, must contain—

(i) the date that the company entered administration, had an administrative receiver appointed or a CVA approved (whichever is the earliest), and

(ii) a statement that the person was a director of the company on that date; and

(d) where the company is in insolvent liquidation, must contain—

(i) the date that the company entered insolvent liquidation, and

(ii) a statement that the person was a director of the company during the 12 months ending with that date.

(4) Notice may in particular be given under this rule—

(a) prior to the insolvent company entering insolvent liquidation where the business (or substantially the whole of the business) is, or is to be, acquired by another company under arrangements made by an office-holder acting in relation to the insolvent company as administrator, administrative receiver or supervisor of a CVA (whether or not at the time of the giving of the notice the person is a director of that other company); or

(b) at a time when the person is a director of another company where—

(i) the other company has acquired, or is to acquire, the whole, or substantially the whole, of the business of the insolvent company under arrangements made by its liquidator, and

(ii) it is proposed that after the giving of the notice a prohibited name should be adopted by the other company.

(5) Notice may not be given under this rule by a person who has already acted in breach of section 216.

Statement as to the effect of the notice under rule 22.4(2)

22.5. The statement as to the effect of the notice under rule 22.4(2) must be as set out below—

"Section 216(3) of the Insolvency Act 1986 lists the activities that a director of a company that has gone into insolvent liquidation may not undertake unless the court gives permission or there is an exception in the Insolvency Rules made under the Insolvency Act 1986. (This includes the exceptions in Part 22 of the Insolvency (England and Wales) Rules 2016.) These activities are—

(a) acting as a director of another company that is known by a name which is either the same as a name used by the company in insolvent liquidation in the 12 months before it entered liquidation or is so similar as to suggest an association with that company;

(b) directly or indirectly being concerned or taking part in the promotion, formation or management of any such company; or

(c) directly or indirectly being concerned in the carrying on of a business otherwise than through a company under a name of the kind mentioned in (a) above.

This notice is given under rule 22.4 of the Insolvency (England and Wales) Rules 2016 where the business of a company which is in, or may go into, insolvent liquidation is, or is to be, carried on otherwise than by the company in liquidation with the involvement of a director of that company and under the same or a similar name to that of that company.

The purpose of giving this notice is to permit the director to act in these circumstances where the company enters (or has entered) insolvent liquidation without the director committing a criminal offence and in the case of the carrying on of the business through another company, being personally liable for that company's debts.

Notice may be given where the person giving the notice is already the director of a company which proposes to adopt a prohibited name."

Second excepted case

22.6.—(1) Where a person to whom section 216 applies as having been a director or shadow director of the liquidating company applies for permission of the court under that section not later than seven business days from the date on which the company went into liquidation, the person may, during the period specified in paragraph (2) below, act in any of the ways mentioned in section 216(3), notwithstanding that the person does not have the permission of the court under that section.

(2) The period referred to in paragraph (1) begins with the day on which the company goes into liquidation and ends either on the day falling six weeks after that date or on the day on which the court disposes of the application for permission under section 216, whichever of those days occurs first.

Third excepted case

22.7. The court's permission under section 216(3) is not required where the company there referred to though known by a prohibited name within the meaning of the section—

(a) has been known by that name for the whole of the period of 12 months ending with the day before the liquidating company went into liquidation; and

(b) has not at any time in those 12 months been dormant within the meaning of section 1169(1), (2) and (3)(a) of the Companies Act(1).

Summary

- The rule against reflective losses is restricted to shareholders and is no longer an impediment to third-party outsiders suing those controlling companies for asset-stripping.

- Asset-stripping is not a recognised tort in itself but may involve one or more torts or breaches of trust including those considered in Chapter 5 including deceit, conspiracy, dishonest assistance or knowing receipt.

- The Insolvency Act 1986 seeks to tackle two incidents of asset stripping outside of an insolvency: s217 will impose personal liability on those who run a new company where they take the name of the old company that has been liquidated; and s423 will give the court powers to grant relief where a company enters into a transaction at a significant undervalue to defraud creditors.

- The OBG tort of unlawful means may potentially be used where an asset-stripper takes a company's assets without engaging the constitutional organs of that company to enter into the transaction voluntarily.

- If there is a judgment there is also potentially a tort of procuring a breach of judgment as was argued in Marex, relying on the principles said to have been recognised in *Lumley v Gye* (1853) 2 E & B 216[246].

- If there is a court order requiring directors to do things, there may also be reason to commit directors or for aiding and abetting a contempt, as considered in the next chapter.

---

[246] Although that case itself appeared to be concerned with procuring a breach of contract, and does not appear to have expressly created any special cause of action relating to breach of judgment.

CHAPTER SEVEN

PERSONAL LIABILITY IN PROCEEDINGS

Introduction

There are two main ways in which liability is imposed by the courts in the context of legal proceedings: first through the exercise of discretionary costs powers, either as security for costs or for costs generally; and second via orders for contempt of court, typically upon committal proceedings being issued.

Directors may be ordered to pay the costs of proceedings involving their company where exceptionally the court considers it just for them to do so, for example because they have derived personal advantage from the litigation or pursued speculative litigation or incurred unreasonable costs by improperly arguing a point. Directors can also be required to pay security for costs.

Those running a company can be personally liable for contempt where they aid and abet a company to commit a breach of court order; or knowingly cause their company to avoid paying a judgment debt or to breach a court order; or do not take reasonable steps to ensure compliance; and they may be criminally responsible for interfering with the course of justice if they deliberately frustrate the purpose of an order[247].

Security for Costs

The courts can require a party other than a claimant to pay security for the defendant's costs under r25.14CPR when satisfied it is just to make such order in all of the circumstances. That

---

[247] See *AG v Punch Ltd* [2003] 1 A.C. 1046.

typically arises where the director has contributed or agreed to contribute to the claimant's costs. As Lord Brown held in *Dymocks Franchise Systems (NSW) v Todd* [2004] 1 W.L.R. 2807 (PC) (costs) at para 25:

> '(3) Where however the non-party not merely funds the proceedings but substantially controls or at any rate is to benefit from them, justice will ordinarily require that if the proceedings fail, he will pay the unsuccessful party's costs. The non party in these cases is not so much facilitating access to justice by the party funded as himself gaining access to justice for his own purposes. He himself is 'the real party' to the litigation.'

A defendant sued by a claimant company of uncertain financial standing may wish to contemplate applying for security for costs not only against the company but also a director. They may wish to can enquire about the funding position and whether a given director is paying their solicitors' costs directly or through the company. They might also try to call for relevant document for example any funding agreement or proof of payments or for any documents relevant to the parties' financial positions. A failure to furnish documents available to a funder can be treated as 'deliberate reticence' and lead to inferences being drawn against the party refusing to furnish the evidence that should readily disprove any point that is being made[248].

Costs generally

The courts have an exceptional jurisdiction to award costs against a non-party under s51 of the Senior Courts Act 1981. An application should involve the non-party first being joined and then being given notice and adequate opportunity to respond.

Such jurisdiction is discretionary [249] and is often invoked in costs applications made against directors of company where such directors are not parties to the proceedings[250]. It is important that any non-party

---

[248] See *SARPD Oil International Ltd v Addax Energy SA* [2016] EWCA Civ 120.
[249] See *Metalloy Supplies Ltd v MA (UK) Ltd* [1997] 1 W.L.R. 1613 at 1620.
[250] See *Aiden Shipping Co Ltd v Interbulk Ltd (the Vimeira) (No 2)* [1986] A.C. 965.

against whom an application for costs is made must be joined as a party under r46.2 CPR and have ample notice of and a chance to give evidence. Joinder is supposed to give the non party all the benefit of having the issues framed and chance to raise matters and have them fairly adjudicated. However, a director only joined after a trial has taken place is often hard pushed disputing findings that have been made, especially if they were on notice of the proceedings and gave evidence or had the opportunity to do so: there can be res judicata[251] especially for the purpose of costs arguments which are ordinarily summarily determined[252]. In that connection, judicial findings can be relied upon if the connection between the non party and the litigation was so close that it would not be unjust to allow such reliance.

Perhaps because of these reasons, courts tend to treat these applications with care and will not permit them to proceed unless non parties have full opportunity to raise issues .It seems a director may possible even have an automatic right of appeal against such order[253].

The courts have a wide discretion and may award costs provided the case is outside of the ordinary course. It is not necessary to show that the director has acted in bad faith, or in abuse of the court's process or involved himself in some other impropriety[254]. There is no general principle however that such a costs order will be appropriate against a director where their conduct is disapproved of because they are responsible for causing costs to be incurred[255]. It is not enough by itself to simply show that the director knows that the company will be unable to meet adverse costs and proceeds regardless[256]. There must be something exceptional in the case making it just to require a non-party

---

[251] See *Bairstow v Secretary of State for Trade and Industry* [2003] EWCA Civ 321 and *Virgin Atlantic Airways Ltd v Premium Aircraft Interiors UK Ltd* [2013] UKSC 46, at paragraphs 17 to 26.

[252] See *Deutsche Bank AG v Sebastian Holdings Inc* [2016] 4 W.L.R. 17, at paras32-34.

[253] See *Land and Property Trust Co (No.3)*, Re [1991] 1 W.L.R. 601; [1991] 3 All E.R. 409.

[254] See *Secretary of State for Trade and Industry v Aurum Marketing Ltd* [2002] B.C.C. 31.

[255] See *Taylor v Pace Developments Ltd* [1991] B.C.C. 406 (Civ), at p409.

[256] See *Goodwood Recoveries Ltd v Breen* [2006] 1 W.L.R. 2723.

to pay the costs. That may be for example because the court considers that the proceedings have been brought or defended improperly, resulting in significant costs being incurred. For example a speculative claim may have been brought[257]. It may be less appropriate to make an order in a case where such a director could have been proceeded against in their own right but were not joined[258].

Cases where such costs orders may be appropriate include situations where: a director substantial stands to benefit and has been personally funding and running the litigation[259]; where they instigate proceedings for some personal advantage rather than for the company's benefit, such as to make money in the interim from postponing the inevitable outcome[260].

The fact that security for costs was ordered will not negate the scope for later making a non-party costs order[261]. This discretion applies not only where a party is unsuccessfully sued, but where they have defended[262] although an application brought by a party that was wrongfully sued and wasted costs may garner greater judicial sympathy[263]

Contempt

If a director knows of a court order requiring a company to do or to refrain from doing something, he may be liable for contempt if he knowingly aids and abets a breach by the company or does something which interferes with the administration of justice by frustrating the effect of an order. Rule 81.4 CPR provide that a committal order may be made against a director of a company where a company is required to do something or disobeys an order. The director will fall under a duty to do

---

[257] See *Goodwood Recoveries Ltd v Breen* [2006] 1 W.L.R. 2723.

[258] See *Symphony Group PLC v Hodgson* [1994] Q.B. 179 (Civ) at pp191-192.

[259] See *Brampton Manor (Leisure) v McLean* [2007] EWHC 3340 (Ch).

[260] See *Secretary of State for Trade and Industry v Aurum Marketing Ltd* [2002] B.C.C. 31.

[261] See *Petromec Inc v Petroleo Brasiliero SA* [2006] EWCA Civ 1038, per Longmore LJ at paras13-14.

[262] See *Taylor v Pace Developments Ltd* [1991] B.C.C. 406 (Civ), at p409.

[263] *Goodwood Recoveries Ltd v Breen* [2006] 1 W.L.R. 2723.

what is reasonable in the circumstances to bring about compliance with the court order: they must take reasonable steps[264]. A director may thus be in breach by failing to do something, even though such inactivity or omission falls short of aiding and abetting[265]. Reasonable steps will likely include doing what is necessary to ensure somebody attends to doing what is required and supervising them to check the order is not overlooked or forgotten[266]

The same principles apply as regards company undertaking given to the court. The director in question thus need not necessarily actively participate in a breach. If they knowingly refuse or fail to do what is reasonable, they can be subject to committal proceedings and held in contempt. What is reasonable in the circumstances will depend on the facts in each case. A director will not be in contempt where a company which cannot afford to pay its way does not comply with an order for payment. Where one director reasonably understands and expects another will effect compliance they will also not be held in contempt[267], and that may more arguably be the case for a non-executive director[268].

A director can also be committed for failing to attend court to provide information about a company's assets and liabilities where an application is made by a judgment creditor requiring an officer of the company to attend – see rule 71.2 CPR.

Summary

- Directors are often liable in proceedings involving their company in costs.

---

[264] See *Public Joint Stock Company, Vseukrainskyi Bank v Sergey Maksimov* [2014] EWHC 3771 Comm at para 27.

[265] See *Biba Ltd v Stratford Investments Ltd* [1973] 1 Ch 281.

[266] See *Lewis v Pontypridd Caerphilly and Newport Railway Co* (1895) 11 TLR 203.

[267] See *Attorney General of Tuvalu v Philatelic Distribution Corp Ltd* [1990] 1 W.L.R. 926.

[268] See *Director General of Fair Trading v Buckland* [1990] 1 W.L.R. 920, at 925.

- They may be made subject to an order requiring them to pay security for the defendant's costs under r25.14 CPR[269].

- They may be liable on a non-party costs under s51 of the <u>Senior Courts Act 1981</u>.

- Such costs liability might arise, for example, where company controllers have derived personal advantage from the litigation[270], or pursued speculative litigation or incurred unreasonable costs by improperly arguing a case[271].

- The non-party will however need to be joined under r46.2 CPR and adequate notice given to ensure an opportunity to respond.

- Also those controlling a company may be committed for contempt of court, for example, where: they have aided and abetted a company to commit a breach of court order; or they knowingly cause their company to avoid paying a judgment debt or to breach a court order; or they do not take reasonable steps to ensure compliance; or they are criminally responsible for interfering with the course of justice for example by deliberately frustrating the purpose of an order[272].

---

[269] See *Dymocks Franchise Systems (NSW) v Todd* [2004] 1 W.L.R. 2807 (PC) (costs) at paras. 24-25.

[270] See *Brampton Manor (Leisure) v McLean* [2007] EWHC 3340 (Ch). See also *Secretary of State for Trade and Industry v Aurum Marketing Ltd* [2002] B.C.C. 31.

[271] See *Goodwood Recoveries Ltd v Breen* [2006] 1 W.L.R. 2723.

[272] See *Attorney General v Punch Ltd* [2003] 1 A.C. 1046.

CHAPTER EIGHT

PERSONAL LIABILITY UNDER STATUTE

Introduction

Acts of Parliament commonly impose personal liability upon those running companies for company activities. Common situations include responsibility under employment law, housing law and tax. There are however plenty of other areas where personal liability also arises including: health and safety law, data protection, and environmental protection law.

Director personal liability can arise also not only in the form of civil liability but personal criminal responsibility. Whilst this book has been primarily concerned with director personal liability to third parties and not with personal criminal responsibility, it is relevant to consider some of the criminal offences imposed personally on directors. For starters, prosecutions can often give rise to compensation orders being made, leading to something that might be not dissimilar to civil recovery. Further, prosecutions can be brought not only by public bodies but also privately by individuals, who might perhaps intentionally seek such compensation orders. And third, there are overlaps and instances where claimants might try to argue that civil personal liability should also arise where there is criminal personal responsibility is provided.

Those seeking to establish civil liability where a statutory duty is imposed giving rise to criminal consequences should beware of the difficulties and risks involved. If a statute does not expressly provide for civil liability, the courts will require considerable persuasion before finding that Parliament intended to confer civil remedies on the grounds that the claimant is within a class of persons whose protection the statute was intended to provide[273]. Cases which have resulted in civil liability for a breach of statutory duty tend to impose specific defined duties, for example under s143 of the Road Traffic Act 1988, or where it is apparent that statute was intended to define or to add to the duty of care arising under the common law[274].

This chapter aims to identify the more common areas encountered in practice where liability may be imposed upon directors, secretaries, employees or officers, and it does so by listing the different areas in summary fashion. This is not intended to be a complete and exhaustive summary of all of the different areas where statute has or might impose personal liability. The legislation is too vast to attempt such endeavour, especially concerning personal criminal responsibility. There are also a lot of well-established specialist texts which already cover a lot of the common situations for example on personal liability relating to director disqualification, tax or health and safety. Instead, this chapter attempts to list the more common areas encountered and in alphabetical order for ease of referencing.

For reader convenience, large tracts of statute have been heavily summarised. Reference is also made below to 'directors' generally whereas often the statute makes specific provision to others not only shadow or de facto directors but also the company secretary or officers or employees. Reliance should not be placed solely on the summation below and the

---

[273] See *X v Bedfordshire CC* [1995] 2 A.C. 633 (HL), which has been doubted: *Phelps v Hillingdon LBC* [2001] 2 A.C. 619. See also *Lonrho Ltd v Shell Petroleum Co Ltd (No.2)* [1982] A.C. 173 where Lord Diplock considered personal liability could arise in two situations namely where it is apparent that the duty was imposed for the benefit of the claimant as an individual or within a class of persons or where the statute created public rights and an individual suffers damage different to the rest of the public.

[274] See the discussion in Charlesworth & Percy on Negligence 14th Ed, Sweet & Maxwell, Consolidated Main work Incorporating Third Supplement, Chapter 13 – Liability for Breach of Statutory Duty. See also Hartley v Rochdale Corp [1908] 2 K.B. 594. per Darling J said: 'I do not think that because there is the power to sue the defendants for penalties they are not liable to be sued for negligence in the doing of the work, provided it be proved that the negligence resulted in injury to a plaintiff.'

primary sources should be consulted in each case, as well as specialist texts and commentary where available.

Bribery and corruption

- A director can be criminally liable for giving or receiving a bribe: s14 Bribery Act 2010.

- A director can be personally liable for consenting to or conniving with their company in giving or receiving a bribe under: ss1, 2, 6, Bribery Act 2010.

- A third party who suffers losses arising out of an impeachable bribe may also be entitled to rescind any contract arising out of it (for example with a company) claim for themselves the bribe or secret commissions (for example received by a director): see *Wood v Commercial First Business Limited* [2021] EWCA Civ 471 (and in particular paragraphs 44 and 92, and 97 to 101).

Company law

- Any officer of the company will commit an offence if they authorise, s119, s350, s429, s790R, s792, s806); disclosing restricted information around takeovers (s949); failing to make trading disclosures (s1054); making false statements (s1112); failing to keep accounting records (s387); failing to declare an interest (s183, s814).

- And subject to s1121, directors of PLCs may, for example, commit offences relating to: the approval procedure (s438); filing accounts and reports (s451); not giving auditor information (ss501, 507), for website publication contraventions (s530).

- Director personal liability can arise civilly for mis-describing a company's assets: s767(3) of the Companies Act 2006.

- personal liability can also arise for failing to observe shareholder rights of pre-emption: see s563 and s568, Companies Act 2006.

- As considered in Chapter 3, a director can be liable on pre-incorporation contracts) under s51 of the Companies Act 1986.

- As considered in Chapter 3, a director can be liable personally for losses caused by failing to comply with trading disclosures including the Companies (Trading Disclosures) Regulations 2008, see Regulation 10.

- Any person that knowingly is party to carrying on a business with an intent to defraud shareholders or creditors commits an offence: s993, Companies Act 2006.

- Directors of PLCs who knowingly contravenes or permits or authorises a contravention of s578 (governing the allotment of shares for subscription) will be liable for any losses caused to third party on an action brought within 2 years: s578, Companies Act 2006.

- A director of a PLC will be jointly and severally liable with the company to repay sums with interest if the company receives sums that are not repaid within 48 hours of a share offer in breach of s578(1) (governing share allocation): see s578(3), Companies Act 2006.

- A director of a PLC commits an offence and can be jointly and severally liable to third parties for losses suffered by reason of the company carrying on a business without a trading certificate being issued: see s761(1) and s767(1) to (3).

Competition law

- A director that causes their company to be part of a cartel involved in price-fixing or market-rigging can be disqualified as well as prosecuted and subject to fines: see s9A-E, Companies Directors Disqualification Act 1986.

- The Competition and Markets Authority also has standing to pursue director disqualifications.

Data protection

- If a director knows of an offence being committed by the company or causes it through their neglect, the director can be guilty of the offence and can be fined personally: s198, <u>Data Protection Act 2018</u>.

Director disqualification

- A disqualified director who is involved in the management of the company will in contravention of an order will be jointly and severally liable: s15, <u>Company Directors Disqualification Act 1986</u>.

- A person who acts on the instruction of somebody who is disqualified or bankrupt involved in running a company will also be personally responsible for relevant debts jointly and severally with the company if he knows about the bankruptcy or disqualification: s15, <u>Company Directors Disqualification Act 1986</u>.

- An undischarged bankrupt or person subject to a bankruptcy restriction order (or undertaking) or a debt relief restriction moratorium or order (or undertaking) will be criminally liable and jointly and severally liable with the company for any liabilities that are incurred whilst they are involved in the management: s11 and 15 the <u>Company Directors Disqualification Act 1986</u>.

Employment law

- A director that harasses or discriminates against an employee can be personally liable together with their company for harassment or discrimination offences: see Employment Appeal Tribunal (EAT) in *Bungay and Paul v Chandel 2011* UKEAT/0331/10/CEA; and <u>Employment Equality (Religion or Belief) Regulations 2003</u>, the principles of which have now been enshrined in the <u>Equality Act 2010</u>.

- Flagrant breaches of an employee's rights can also give rise to personal liability on the part of the director for procuring a breach of employment contract in bad faith: see *Antzuzis v DJ Houghton Catching Services* [2019] EWHC 843 (QB).

Environmental law

- Section 34 of the Environmental Protection Act 1990 imposes a duty of care on anyone handling controlled waste (with a more limited application to householders concerning domestic household waste) to take all reasonable steps.

- There are a plethora of environmental law offences too vast to list here that any person can commit but it is relevant to note that many of them give rise to directors being criminally liable where they consent, connive or through their default cause their company to commit an environmental offence.

- Also false 'greenwashing claims' by directors may well result in personal liability. The move to make Environmental, Social and Governance (ESG) reporting mandatory may give rise to directors issuing increasing claims about their company's green credentials. Actions for deceit may well become more common as well as claims under s90 and/or s90A Financial Markets and Services Act 2000. Consumer Protection from Unfair Trading Regulations 2008 and/or advertising law and/or competition law may also all be relevant in grounding causes of action[275].

False accounting

- Personal criminal liability can be imposed on directors that know, permit or willingly ignore false accounting: ss17-18 of the Theft Act 1968.

---

[275] See the Competition and Markets Authority: Green Claims Code, London, published 20 September 2021.

Financial Services

- Whilst authorised and regulated firms, typically have deep pockets and insurance and so often make better defendants, professional negligence claims can be brought against the particular negligent individuals in accordance with ordinary common law principles provided there has been sufficient assumption of responsibility.

- False representations by directors in a prospectus or other documents produced to procure investment can give rise to personal liability and not only in the tort of deceit, but for negligent mis-statement: see *Possfund Custodian Trustee Ltd v Diamond* [1996] 1 W.L.R. 1351.

- Compensation is payable by 'any person responsible' for causing another to suffer losses as a result of any untrue statements in a prospectus or in listing particulars: s90 Financial Markets and Services Act 2000, but see also the exclusions and defences, including reasonable belief in a statement's veracity upon making reasonable enquiries[276].

- A statutory tort will be committed by any person who issues an untrue statement knowing or being reckless about the error, omits information officially required, knowing the omission to be dishonest concealment or dishonestly delay publishing officially required information.

- A director can be liable in the tort of deceit for making dishonest representations causing losses according to the common law principles.

- Penalties for market abuse are imposed for insider trading which may involve a director: s118, Financial Markets and Services Act 2000.

---

[276] See Financial Markets and Services Act 2000, s86, s90ZA, s90(2) and (5) schedule 10; also Financial Services and Markets Act 2000 (Official Listing of Securities) Regulation 2001; and the FCA Handbook Prospectus Rules.

- In addition to common law principles for upholding personal liability, a principal and not only an appointed representative can be personally liable for business for which the principal has accepted responsibility: s39, Financial Markets and Services Act 2000.

Fraud offences

- Personal liability can be imposed upon company officers that know, permit or willingly ignore any fraud offence under the Fraud Act 2006, under s12 thereof and see ss2–3.

- It is an offence also to make a false statement of the affairs of the company to deceive creditors – s19, Theft Act 1968.

Health & Safety

- A director which consents to or through their default causes a company to breach health and safety law can be criminally personally liable: see s37 of the Health and Safety at Work etc Act 1974.

- A director may also be disqualified for H&S breaches under s2(1) of the Company Directors Disqualification Act 1986.

Housing

- An officer will commit an offence if their company commits an offence under the Housing Act 2004 with their 'consent, connivance or neglect': s251, Housing Act 2004 for example where they were 'well aware of what was going on and agreed' (consent), or were they were 'equally aware of what was going but his agreement was tacit, not actively encouraging what happened but letting it continue and saying nothing about it' (connivance) or 'omitted/ neglected to do something which he ought to have done' (neglect)[277].

---

[277] See *Huckerby v Elliott* [1970] 1 All ER 189; and for neglect see *HMRC v O'Rourke* [2013] UKUT 49 (TCC): it does not involve a subjective element with actual

- Directors can also be personally liable for civil financial penalties imposed under s249A of the Housing Act 2004 in cases of consent, connivance or neglect notwithstanding that the enactment does not explicitly impose personal liability and for such cases 'there is no additional requirement that the company must also have been charged or convicted'[278].

- However, a director cannot be liable on an action for a rent repayment order unless they are the landlord[279].

Insolvency

- Where a company becomes insolvent a director may be liable for wrongful or fraudulent trading under ss213-214 of the Insolvency Act 1986 and this may result in them being pursued personally for funds to pay to the company creditors generally. Whilst such cases can only be brought by the insolvency practitioner office holder such claims are capable of being assigned to third parties including creditors after 1 October 2015 under ss246ZA-ZB, Insolvency Act 1986, and so too are claims for general director liability for misfeasance of for preferences.

- As considered in Chapter 6, a creditor can personally claim losses from a director under s217 who in contravention of s216 of the Insolvency Act 1986 becomes involved in the management of a new company reusing the name of a liquidated company.

---

knowledge of the contravention, which in that case, was that tax had not been paid, but the ordinary objective test applicable where neglect or negligence is in issue.

[278] See *Sutton v Norwich City Council* [2020] UKUT 90 (LC).

[279] See *Rakusen v Jepson* [2021] EWCA Civ 1150; also, see *Kaszowska v White* [2022] UKUT 11 (LC) per the Deputy President of the Lands Chamber, Martin Rodger QC, on s40(2) of the Housing and Planning Act 2016: 'The only person against whom section 40(2) permits a rent repayment order to be made is a landlord. Had it been intended to extend the scope of rent repayment orders to company directors Parliament would surely have said so in explicit terms.'

- Personal liability can accrue to a person involved in the running of a company who has, during its insolvency, 'misapplied or retained, or become accountable for, any money or other property of the company, or been guilty of any misfeasance or breach of any fiduciary or other duty in relation to the company' and such person can be liable to restore or compensate the company on an action brought not only by insolvency practitioner but potentially a creditor.

- A director who continues to trade following the presentation of a winding up petition without obtaining a validation order exposes himself not only to action for wrongful trading or misfeasance by a subsequent liquidator, but potentially to actions for breach of warrant of authority as any disposition by a company without a validation order is void: s127, Insolvency Act 1986.

Manslaughter

- Companies and individuals are subject to common law offence of manslaughter by gross negligence: *R v Adomako* [1994] 3 All ER 79.

Pensions

- A person who is party to, or knowingly assists an employer to avoid paying a debt under s75 of the Pensions Act 1995 on the winding up of a scheme can be liable upon a contribution notice served by the Pensions Regulator.

Recruitment companies

- Directors of recruitment agency companies can also be personally liable for their companies failing to account to HMRC to evade employment taxes: Regulation 97ZA, Income Tax (Pay As You Earn) Regulations 2003.

<u>Tax</u>

- Company directors can be jointly and severally liable with the company for tax liabilities and tax debts, particularly in cases of tax avoidance or insolvency. There is an entire regime governing joint and several liability notices: see s100, <u>Finance Act 2020</u>, and Schedule 13, which is especially relevant where:

  o a company has gone into liquidation for a third time and the same director or directors have been in charge within the last five years and there is tax debt of at least £10,000 which is more than 50% of the other unsecured creditors; or

  o where the company has entered into tax avoidance arrangements or has engaged in tax evasive conduct; or where the company is subject to an insolvency procedure, or

  o there is a serious possibility of it becoming subject to one; or where the individual was responsible for the company's conduct which they took part in, facilitated or assisted or from which they knowingly benefited; or

  o where there is or is likely to be, a tax liability relating to the tax-avoidance arrangements or to the tax-evasive conduct; or

  o where there is a serious possibility some or all of this tax liability will not be paid.

- personal liability can arise for evasion of VAT or other tax liabilities including not paying betting or gaming duties due under the <u>Betting and Gaming Duties Act 1981</u>

- A failure to pay national insurance contributions attributable to the fraud or neglect of a director can give rise to personal liability: s121C, <u>the Social Security Administration Act 1992</u>.

CHAPTER NINE

CONCLUSIONS: THE IMPLICATIONS FOR PRACTITIONERS

Practitioners will be able to draw out of the discussion above the following points:

- Contract law does not give rise to any liability for corporate agents on a company contract provided the company is the proper party to the contract.

- All too often, however, directors fail to comply with the company trading disclosures[280] with the result that it may be more difficult for them to prove that their company was the proper party to the contract and/or criminal offences are committed under s84 Companies Act 2006 and/or the company will be at risk of being unable to enforce its contract either on a claim or counterclaim pursuant to s83 Companies Act 2006.

- Sometimes, persons promoting a company they intend to form do not realise they cannot contract in its name until incorporated. Under s51 of the Companies Act 2006 persons promoting a company they plan to form will be personally liable on any contracts they purport to arrange for the company.

- Post-incorporation where those running a company do not give enough notice of the company's existence or involvement so as to

---

[280] See Company, Limited Liability Partnership and Business (Trading Disclosures) Regulations 2015 SI 2015/17 and also Companies (Trading Disclosures) Regulations 2008.

make the company the proper party to the contract, then those negotiating the contract risk being personally liable upon it.

- Who the proper party to the contract is will be a question of construction which will be an objective assessment when dealing with written contracts.

- For oral contracts and/or for part-oral and part-written contracts, it will be a question of fact who the third-party outsider subjectively intended to contract with[281].

- An agent will not be liable for causing his or her principal to breach a contract under the tort of procuring a breach of contract unless he or she acted in bad faith to their principal.

- If a director purposefully breaches a company's contract he or she will not be personally liable to a third party contracting with the company which suffers harm provided they act within their authority to the company and the company is the proper party to the contract (and they have not entered into another agreement in their own right, such as a personal guarantee).

- Where the company is or appears on the face of things to be the proper party to a contract or to own property in the company's own name, veil-piercing or veil-lifting may be relevant, in accordance with the principles of concealment or evasion.

- Lifting the veil will be appropriate where upon careful scrutiny the Court can be satisfied that the true position underlying the transaction is that the controller and not the company is the proper party for example because the transaction putatively in favour of the company is a sham or the company is the controller's agent or nominee holding on trust.

---

[281] See Article 101 of Bowstead and Reynolds on Agency, Sweet & Maxwell, 22nd Ed citing *Holding v Elliott* (1860) 5 H. & N. 117.

- Piercing the veil may be appropriate where there is an existing restriction or liability that is being evaded by the subsequent interposition of a company but it should only be resorted to where other relationships, principles or causes of action are unavailable.

- Outside of a contractual context, the important question is whether an outside third party harmed by somebody running a company can prove they were involved in committing or commissioning some cause of action.

- It seems that most causes of action will be available to a third-party outsider and not merely those involving fraud or an economic tort. Directors can also be personally liable on other common law or equitable causes of action.

- Directors can be liable amongst other things in negligence causing harm to property or person, or for nuisance, or for waste, or in equity for knowing receipt or dishonest assistance.

- Claims to recover pure economic losses for negligence will be subject to the special assumption of responsibility test.

- In cases of conversion of property being dealt with by the company, there typically needs to be control of the goods and denial of the true owner's claim or the director will commission the conversion by being involved in bringing it about in bad faith[282].

- If all of the elements of a tort cannot be made out against an individual director, it may be possible to prove they commissioned it by being sufficiently involved in it to be a joint tortfeasor.

---

[282] See Article 114, Bowstead and Reynolds on Agency, Sweet & Maxwell, 22nd Ed and *Thunder Air Ltd v Hilmarsson* [2008] EWHC 355 (Ch) and *Caparo Industries Plc v Dickman* [1990] 2 A.C. 605 at 638C-E.

- Joint tortfeasorship can arise in instances where one instigates another to commit a tort or where they both share a common design to bring it about.

- Stripping a company of assets to defraud a third party might give rise not only to claims in conspiracy, but on an action based on the unlawful means tort.

- The Insolvency Act 1986 also covers asset-stripping in phoenix situations where a liquidating company's name is re-used and also in cases where the company transfers assets to controllers at an undervalue to prejudice creditors.

- Directors can also become personally liable in civil proceedings involving their company where it is appropriate to make a security for costs order or non-party costs order or where they commit a contempt of court for example by aiding and abetting a company to commit a breach of court order; or knowingly causing their company to avoid paying a judgment debt; or they not taking reasonable steps to ensure compliance with orders; or they are criminally responsible for interfering with the course of justice for example by deliberately frustrating the purpose of an order[283].

- There are also sorts of other statute which impose personal liability on controllers, including in housing, tax, data protection, and environmental law.

- Statute may make express provision for civil liability or it may be possible to argue that criminal liability was also intended to create an actionable civil liability where it can be shown that Parliament intended to protect the claimant by creating the duty.

---

[283] See *Attorney General v Punch Ltd* [2003] 1 A.C. 1046.

- The fact directors may be personally liable on so many causes of action, does not detract however from the difficulties in establishing liability.

- Often decisions will be made in small companies without any formal minuting being produced recording decisions made at formally convened meetings. Practitioners may thus be hard pushed formulating and advancing claims with such informational asymmetry.

- Practitioners would thus want to consider the array of disclosure levers at their disposal including through resort to voluntary pre-action correspondence, pre-action disclosure applications or subject access data requests.

MORE BOOKS BY
LAW BRIEF PUBLISHING

A selection of our other titles available now:-

'A Practical Guide to Document Signing and Electronic Signatures for Conveyancers' by Lorraine Richardson
'A Practical Guide to Transgender Law' by Robin Moira White & Nicola Newbegin
'Artificial Intelligence – The Practical Legal Issues (2nd Edition)' by John Buyers
'A Practical Guide to Residential Freehold Conveyancing' by Lorraine Richardson
'A Practical Guide to Pensions on Divorce for Lawyers' by Bryan Scant
'A Practical Guide to Challenging Sham Marriage Allegations in Immigration Law' by Priya Solanki
'A Practical Guide to Legal Rights in Scotland' by Sarah-Jane Macdonald
'A Practical Guide to New Build Conveyancing' by Paul Sams & Rebecca East
'A Practical Guide to Defending Barristers in Disciplinary Cases' by Marc Beaumont
'A Practical Guide to Inherited Wealth on Divorce' by Hayley Trim
'A Practical Guide to Practice Direction 12J and Domestic Abuse in Private Law Children Proceedings' by Rebecca Cross & Malvika Jaganmohan
'A Practical Guide to Confiscation and Restraint' by Narita Bahra QC, John Carl Townsend, David Winch
'A Practical Guide to the Law of Forests in Scotland' by Philip Buchan
'A Practical Guide to Health and Medical Cases in Immigration Law' by Rebecca Chapman & Miranda Butler
'A Practical Guide to Bad Character Evidence for Criminal Practitioners by Aparna Rao
'A Practical Guide to Extradition Law post-Brexit' by Myles Grandison et al
'A Practical Guide to Hoarding and Mental Health for Housing Lawyers' by Rachel Coyle
'A Practical Guide to Psychiatric Claims in Personal Injury – 2nd Edition' by Liam Ryan
'Stephens on Contractual Indemnities' by Richard Stephens

Printed in Great Britain
by Amazon

42787285R00086